IRAQ

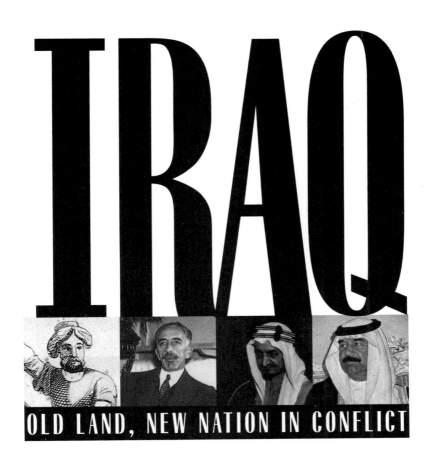

IRAQ

OLD LAND, NEW NATION IN CONFLICT

William Spencer

Twenty-First Century Books
Brookfield, Connecticut

Published by Twenty-First Century Books
A Division of The Millbrook Press, Inc.
2 Old New Milford Road
Brookfield, Connecticut 06804
www.millbrookpress.com

Photographs courtesy of Corbis: pp. 16 (© Caroline Penn), 43 (© Françoise de Mulder); The Bridgeman Art Library/British Museum, London, UK: p. 19; NGS Image Collection: pp. 20 (Photo Archive Submitter), 94 (Steve McCurry), 124 (Sisse Brimberg); Corbis-Bettmann: p. 22; North Wind Picture Archives: pp. 24, 36; Corbis/Bettmann-UPI: pp. 70, 76, 84; Hulton Getty/Liaison Agency: p. 63; Sygma: p. 105 (© Les Stone); Corbis/Reuters: p. 106. Maps by Jeff Ward.

Library of Congress Cataloging-in-Publication Data
Spencer, William, 1922-
Iraq: old land, new nation in conflict/William Spencer.
p. cm.
Includes bibliographical references and index.
Summary: Traces the history of Iraq, from its Mesopotamian origins
to its current political turbulence and its crises with international relations.
ISBN 0-7613-1356-7 (lib. bdg.)
1. Iraq—History. [1. Iraq—History.] I. Title.
DS70.62.S64 2000 956.7—dc21 99-049894

CONTENTS

IRAQ

UP UNTIL the last decades of the twentieth century, most Americans knew little about a small country called Iraq. It was far away, and difficult to locate on a world map. Nor could they identify its leader or describe its form of government or political system or any other essential facts about the country. The country had no relevance to the daily lives of most of us. During the 1980s, Iraq drew some attention from the U.S. media due to a bloody war with its neighbor Iran, which was better known because of its location as the setting for the occupation of our embassy and the holding there of American hostages for 444 days.

But since 1990, Iraq's president and national leader, Saddam Hussein, has become a familiar name in most American households and a popular subject for news analysts and political cartoonists. More important, he and his country represent an ongoing foreign policy problem not only for the United States but also for other countries in the Middle East as well as the international community. The problem emerged when Iraqi forces invaded and

9

occupied its neighbor, the independent state of Kuwait, in defiance of the rules of international law governing the relations of nations to each other. Although the Iraqis were driven out of Kuwait by the armies of an international coalition of nations, the subsequent discovery that the country was developing a secret arsenal of chemical, biological, and nuclear weapons has compounded the problem.

The United Nations (UN) continues to regard the Iraqi weapons program as a threat to world peace. After the 1991 Gulf War ended with the expulsion of Iraqi forces from Kuwait, a UN inspection team which included several American weapons disposal experts went to Iraq to locate and destroy the country's "weapons of mass destruction" as they are called in international relations language. Despite a lack of cooperation on the Iraqi side, they were able to carry out a major portion of their work. In December 1998, however, the Iraqi government ordered them to leave. Since that time there has been no direct monitoring of the weapons program. In December 1999, Iraq refused to admit inspectors from the International Atomic Energy Agency (IAEA), a UN agency responsible for verification of the uranium stockpiles of countries (including Iraq) which had signed the 1968 Nuclear Non-Proliferation Treaty. In January 2000, however, they were readmitted.

Due to its aggressive actions toward its neighbors and its noncooperation with the UN, Iraq is considered by most countries to be an "outlaw nation," one that does not follow the rules of behavior expected of nations in their dealings with each other. As a result this nation the size of California with a population of 22 million has become a major player in the drama of international relations.

After Iraq had been driven out of Kuwait the Bush and then the Clinton administrations took the lead in punishing it for its violations of international law. The method chosen has been that of sanctions, by which a nation's right to trade freely with others, export its products, and import materials and supplies needed for its population in its national development, is severely restricted. The sanctions were imposed originally in 1991. They were eased in part in 1996 under the UN-approved "oil-for-food" program, which allows Iraq to sell oil in order to pay for imports of food, medical supplies, and other commodities needed by its people. This program has lessened the impact of the sanctions on the Iraqis. Although there is increasing disagreement among the members of the Security Council as to the effectiveness of the sanctions, thus far they have been renewed every six months, with the U.S. insisting on conclusive proof that Iraq's weapons have been destroyed before they are lifted.

Iraq is also considered an outlaw nation in the sense that its government mistreats and represses its own people, particularly those whose ethnic, linguistic, or religious background is different from that of the ruling elite. This mistreatment reached such a high level in the late 1980s and after the Gulf War that large sections of the country were placed under international control. As a result, for all practical purposes Iraqi sovereignty is limited to about one-third of its territory.

These matters and the present status of Iraq in the world of nations will be examined in more detail in the chapters that follow. But it is important to note at the outset that Iraq has been in existence as a nation, in the modern sense of the term, for less than three-quarters of a century, while its authoritarian leader has held absolute power for only two decades. Like many other nations of the Middle East and Africa, Iraq is a product of twentieth-century international politics and the colonial policies of European powers. But the history of the land of Iraq goes back some 8,000 years. In its ancient form as Mesopotamia it was literally the cradle of civilization. An understanding of

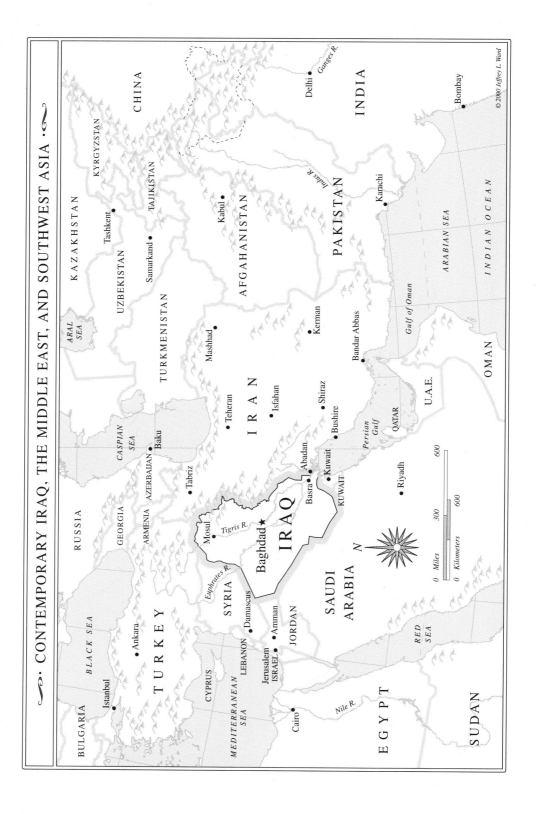

CONTEMPORARY IRAQ, THE MIDDLE EAST, AND SOUTHWEST ASIA

© 2000 Jeffrey L. Ward

this long and rich history and the role of the past in shaping the modern Iraqi nation are essential not only to world leaders and policymakers but also to young Americans who are coming to adulthood in the twenty-first century.

The Iraqi heritage is a proud one. Iraqi ancestors made such contributions to our modern world as a written language, agriculture and the growing of food crops, the building of cities and the urban environment, basic systems of government, and a religious structure centered on gods and goddesses guiding human affairs.

Iraq's people have a share in this proud heritage. At the same time they are struggling with the problems of building a modern nation. One could say that they have an identity problem, that of deciding who they are. Are they Iraqis, patriotic citizens of a particular nation, or clansmen or tribesmen responsible to no law above that of the clan or tribe? Whatever his faults as a national leader, Saddam Hussein has made serious efforts to build a sense of national pride in his people, restoring such monuments of their past as the great Mesopotamian city of Babylon to remind them of their long-ago glories. In the process, he has identified himself as the modern protector of his country and its link with its brilliant past. Saddam fancies himself as a modern-day Nebuchadnezzar (the greatest of the Babylonian kings), and his gleaming white palace on Saddam Hill overlooking the ruins reminds Iraqis daily of their hero and benefactor.

Pride in this heritage, in the glories of the Arab nation of the past, and a determination to play the role of power broker in the region based on Iraq's wealth and resources are key elements in the world-view of Saddam Hussein. It is a narrow world-view and one based on a set of miscalculations that have brought suffering and great hardship to his people. But it is a world-view very different from that of American foreign-policy makers. The Israeli scholar-diplomat Abba Eban reminds us that "all Ameri-

14 can governments make their decisions in terms of the national interest and of moral highmindedness. As the repository of the principle of liberty, America found it natural to interpret the security provided by great oceans as a sign of divine providence, and to attribute its actions to superior moral insight."[1] Iraq, in common with its Mesopotamian ancestors, never enjoyed this luxury (of the protection of oceans).

In a speech after the defeat of his armies in the Gulf War, Saddam Hussein told his people: "The resistance of our heroes to the warplanes and rockets of aggression is the strongest indication of the steadfastness in the hearts of Iraqis and their great readiness not to give up the role given them by God." In other speeches he refers frequently to a time of greatness for Iraq even before "the Arabs as a people whom we know today did not live in the land between the rivers."[2] Admittedly Iraq's development into a modern nation with a particular national identity is incomplete, marked by frequent violence and deep divisions between its various population groups and currently subject to the enormous ego of its national leader. But as we look back over its long history, the modern Iraqi nation begins to illustrate this well-known description: "A nation is a soul, a spiritual principle, a common glory in the past, a common hope for the future. To have done great things together, to work to do them again—these are the conditions for the existence of a nation."[3]

CHAPTER ONE

LAND BETWEEN THE RIVERS

LONG BEFORE there was a kingdom or a republic of Iraq, there was a vast rolling land, crossed by two mighty rivers and flanked by high rugged mountains. Its inhabitants called it simply "the land"—it was all they knew or cared about, and they had no idea what lay beyond the horizon. We call this land Mesopotamia, a word that has come down to us from ancient languages meaning "land between the rivers." These rivers, the Tigris and Euphrates, rise in the north, in what is today Turkey, and flow downstream (southward) until they join and empty into the Persian Gulf. These rivers were the lifeblood of Mesopotamia. They provided water for the growing of food crops and the resulting settlement of wandering groups of humans in villages that eventually grew into towns and cities.

Modern Iraq is physically different from ancient Mesopotamia, with its cities of skyscraper buildings, paved roads, oil derricks, and other features of twentieth-century civilization. But the countryside is still dominated by desert and mountain, river and flat plain. Where the Tigris

15

Modern Baghdad looks like many other cities.

and Euphrates join there is a wide delta, not unlike the Mississippi River delta north of New Orleans, which enters the Persian Gulf through a watery bay called the Shatt al-Arab, where huge tankers formerly departed with oil to foreign markets.

Some 5,000 years ago, when wandering peoples settled in southern Mesopotamia, the land between the rivers seemed to them an ideal place to settle down. Although it has very little rainfall and is unbearably hot in the long summers, the soil was (and is) fertile, and there is plenty of water from the rivers. The plains were covered with grasses for the flocks of sheep and goats of the settlers, and the marshes abounded with fish. The area must have seemed a true paradise, a Garden of Eden not unlike the one described in the Book of Genesis in the Bible.

This combination of geography and natural resources encouraged human settlement in permanent houses and agriculture, the growing of food crops. Mesopotamia was one of the first areas of the world where agriculture was practiced on a regular basis. Abundant water from the Tigris and Euphrates encouraged the development of irrigation, the science of growing crops in areas with little or no rainfall. Before long Mesopotamian farmers were not only growing enough food for their communities but also producing surpluses. As a result they began trading with nearby communities and then with distant peoples. Mesopotamia became the center for trade across the Middle East, and over many decades villages grew into market towns and eventually into cities.

From archaeological excavations we know the names of many of these cities and a good deal about how people lived in them. The most important of these early cities were Sumer, Akkad, Uruk, Eridu, "Ur of the Chaldees," from which Abraham departed to found a new nation for his people in Canaan (later Palestine, now Israel). In Sumer the world's first written language was developed, due to Mesopotamia's importance as a global trading center. The Sumerian language was cuneiform, with wedge-shaped letters rather than pictures representing words as in the Chinese and Egyptian languages. Sumerian was a business-oriented language, inscribed on stone tablets, with a system of seals to identify ownership of goods much like cattle branding. This first "world language" has vanished and survives only in the stone tablets discovered by archaeologists. But one writer has suggested after a visit to the marshes near the site of ancient Sumer that "some Iraqis still have a touch of the Sumerian in them."[4]

The second major contribution of Mesopotamia to present-day civilization was the development of a political system. It was based on the city as an independent unit, a city-state. Each of these ancient cities was the home of a god, sacred to him (and sometimes her, for long before Judaism and Christianity, with their emphasis on a patriarchal god, Middle Eastern peoples respected and believed in the power of goddesses along with their male gods). Because it was the home of a god, the Mesopotamian city was a sacred place. Each city had its society of priests, who took care of the temples and other sacred buildings honoring a local god or goddess.

Over the centuries certain city-states came to dominate others, and in the twenty-fourth century B.C. one local ruler, Sargon of Akkad, assumed the title of king and became the overlord of neighboring cities. Sargon also extended his authority over large parts of what are today Iran, Syria, and Turkey, and he is considered the first imperial ruler, in the sense of ruling over a large territory inhabited by many different peoples.

The development of a written language, with permanent record-keeping on clay tablets for business transactions, contributed to the rise of an urban-based civilization. Sargon appointed local governors for the cities in his realm, with a cadre of officials (a bureaucracy, in the modern sense of the term) to manage local government. The priests made up another power group, who were important due to their role as agents or representatives of the gods. A merchant class came into existence to manage commerce and business, while skilled engineers set up and ran the all-important irrigation system that made agriculture possible in this arid land. The amazing thing about these "technical experts" is that they were able to build a complicated system of canals with locks and sluices for irrigation using only the most basic tools 5,000 years ago! Working with bricks, clay, straw, and other natural materials, they mastered such architectural techniques as the barrel vault, the corbel, the arch, and the dome long before the Greeks, Romans, and other peoples came to use them.

This Mesopotamian world map depicts the campaign of King Sargon of Akkad in the twenty-fourth century B.C.

The unique Mesopotamian contribution to architecture was the *ziggurat*. The exact meaning of the word is uncertain, but it describes the particular structure that was the home of the god in each Mesopotamian city. Ziggurats are somewhat similar to modern skyscrapers, in that they rise from a broad base to a narrow summit, like the Empire State Building in New York City. They are not nearly as tall as skyscrapers, however. Each ziggurat has a broad rectangular platform at its base, with two similar but narrower platforms above it. At the top is a small tower, the shrine of the god on earth. Broad stairways lead upward from the terraces or platforms to the summit. Most scholars believe that the ziggurats were meant to link earth with heaven, enabling the god to travel directly from his (or her) earthly home to a permanent residence

In the 1920s the Great Ziggurat at Ur was excavated. The ziggurat measures more than 200 feet (61 meters) in length and 150 feet (46 meters) in width.

above the clouds. Standing at the top of a ziggurat, such as the Great Ziggurat at Ur, most of which is still above ground due to excavation, one can look down from several hundred feet above the flat Mesopotamian plain and feel "at home" with the gods.[5]

BABYLON AND THE RULE OF LAW

The ruins of Babylon, a half-hour drive from modern Baghdad, the capital of Iraq, have been excavated over the years by archaeologists, and they underscore its importance as a world capital thirty-five centuries ago. Babylon's greatest contribution to our modern world, however, was not in bricks or mortar. In the eighteenth millennium B.C. a line of kings from Babylon came to rule most of southern Mesopotamia and adjoining lands. One of these kings was named Hammurabi. He ruled for forty-two years, during which he wrote the code of laws that bears his name, the first such law code in human history.

The Code of Hammurabi was written in the Sumerian script called cuneiform. There are 282 laws in all, inscribed on huge steles (pillars), which were originally placed at strategic points in Hammurabi's kingdom. They begin with a blessing on all who obey them and end with a curse, the king's personal warning, on those who disregard them. To some extent the code is based on an "eye for an eye, a tooth for a tooth" philosophy. Thus, if a house is so poorly constructed that it collapses and kills its owner, the builder is liable and may be put to death. But other rulings deal with problems familiar to us today, such as marriage and family relations, property, robbery and other crimes, the minimum wage (for a day's work), the purchase and sale of slaves and their owners' obligations toward them, and the fees that may be charged by doctors, lawyers, and accountants.

This relief of Hammurabi before the sun-god is from one of the steles on which the law code is inscribed.

Hammurabi's code did not lead to the establishment of a formal legal system with courts, judges, and juries as we have today, but his rulings clearly point toward such a system. The steles on which he inscribed them may be seen in museums, but the Babylon he ruled and lived in is buried far underground. The Babylon of Saddam Hussein's reconstruction is much later, during the reign of King Nebuchadnezzar (604–562 B.C.). This celebrated ruler brought most of the land between the rivers under his control in a compact Babylonian kingdom. His armies also campaigned far afield. One such campaign resulted in the capture of Jerusalem. The victorious Babylonians brought back some 7,000 warriors as captives, all the able-bodied men of the city, plus several thousand artisans and craftsmen to be employed in the beautification of his capital.

In addition to his military skills and wise leadership, Nebuchadnezzar was a great builder. He gave special attention to Babylon, and workers and craftsmen under his personal direction soon made it into one of the most beautiful cities in the ancient world. It was built in the form of a square, 56 miles (90 kilometers) in circumference and encircled by a deep moat filled with water and triple walls each measuring 50 cubits wide by 200 cubits high. (A cubit is an ancient measurement of length, from the tip of the middle finger to the point of the elbow.) There were guard towers at each of the four corners of the walls. The inner city contained palaces, temples, the ziggurat of Marduk (the city's main god), and the famed Hanging Gardens, one of the seven wonders of the ancient world. The gardens consisted of a series of stone terraces built on earth brought from outside Babylon and piled up so that it resembled a small mountain—the topmost terrace being level with the top of the outside walls. Diodorus Siculus wrote that these terraces "were thickly planted with trees of every kind, with earth deep enough to nourish their roots, while the topmost terrace had hidden machines for supplying water, raising the water in great abundance from the river, although no one outside could see it done."[6]

The famous Hanging Gardens—one of the seven wonders of the ancient world.

THE WOLVES OF ASSYRIA

The northern part of Mesopotamia, extending from the Tigris plain northward into the mountains of Kurdistan, was in ancient times called Assyria. The Assyrian story brings us to Old Testament times. Armies from Assyria invaded Palestine in the eighth century B.C. and carried off the ten northern tribes of Israelites into captivity, never to be heard from again. They also besieged Jerusalem, prompting these famous lines by the nineteenth-century English poet Lord Byron:

> "The Assyrian came down like a wolf on the fold
> And his cohorts were gleaming in purple and gold."

The Assyrians took their name from the god Ashur, worshiped along with his female counterpart Ishtar by many Mesopotamians. Their first capital, named for him, was their main religious center until the establishment of their imperial capital of Nineveh, the "evil city" regularly denounced by Old Testament prophets for its wickedness.

Although the Assyrians were long established in northern Mesopotamia, they did not become a factor in Middle Eastern power struggles until the ninth century B.C. The founder of their empire was Ashurnasirpal II (883–859 B.C.). His realm reached from Lebanon on the Mediterranean coast to the mountains of northwest Iran. In order for later peoples to remember him, he left his mark on clay tablets, describing his campaigns. On one tablet he wrote: "The fear of my dominion reached to Babylonia; the terror of my weapons overwhelmed all."

The image of Assyria as a state geared for war was enhanced by Sennacherib (704–681 B.C.). In addition to the conquest of Israel and the siege of Jerusalem, he captured and destroyed much of Babylon, digging canals under its walls to undermine their foundations and carrying off most of the population as slaves. But Sennacherib's fame rests on the establishment of Nineveh as Assyria's imperial capital. It was surrounded by 8 miles (13 kilometers) of walls, wide enough at the top for three chariots to ride abreast. At its center was the royal palace, with a huge park filled with orchards, rare plants such as myrrh (brought from far-off Arabia), spice plants, and vines. Water was brought from rivers 30 miles (48 kilometers) away to irrigate these gardens, and long before the Romans designed the aqueduct to carry water from distant places down to supply their cities, Nineveh had its own aqueduct to provide a permanent water supply.

Not unlike the modern Iraqi nation, Assyria depended upon its army for the defense and support of its rulers. The Assyrian army was probably the world's first standing army. Conquered peoples were allowed to serve in its units, and each ethnic group kept its own weapons, dress, customs, and identity. The army also had specialized units, such as axmen, slingers, archers, and cavalry. There were even specialists in siege warfare who would erect battering-rams for use against besieged cities or bridges of boats for river crossings. All in all, the Assyrian army was the most formidable force in the region in its day.

The Assyrians also used what we would call psychological warfare against their enemies. Their rulers believed that Ashur had given them a "divine mission" to subdue their neighbors. Thus, during the siege of Jerusalem, Sennacherib sent a message, in Hebrew, to the population of the city, warning them of the uselessness of resistance. The message ended with these prophetic words: "Has any of the gods of the nations ever delivered his land out of the hand of the King of Assyria?" Another Assyrian ruler described his treatment of captured enemy soldiers in grim terms: "Many of them I burned in fire. Many I took alive; I cut off their hands, their noses, their ears."

Yet the Assyrians made some positive contributions to Mesopotamian life. They developed many of the region's natural resources—grain, timber, and bitumen (a tarlike substance), for example—and this development of resources was important in linking together the various regions of the Middle East into a trading unit. The Assyrians built and maintained a network of imperial roads, with a postal service of carriers on fleet horses or camels to provide rapid communications between the cities and towns of their empire. Also it was their policy to move conquered peoples from their original homes to other areas, on the theory that displacement would discourage resistance. But in the long run this policy helped to break down ethnic and cultural barriers, replacing a narrow group identity with a larger cultural one. The modern Iraqis, like other Middle Eastern peoples today, have benefited from this cultural mixing, which is essential in the building of a nation out of many different social, linguistic, religious, and other components.

INVASIONS AND FOREIGN RULE

Nebuchadnezzar's Babylonian kingdom would prove to be the last home-grown government in Mesopotamia for ages to come. Henceforth until the establishment of the twentieth-century kingdom of Iraq, the destiny of the land between the rivers passed into the hands of outsiders. In 539 B.C., Cyrus, a Persian chief who had united the Medes and Persians under his leadership, captured Babylon. Mesopotamia became a province of the vast Persian empire built by Cyrus and his successors. It was a genuine land empire, stretching from Egypt across the Middle East to the western border of India.

For a brief period Mesopotamian peoples benefited from the "king's peace" that blanketed this vast territory. The irrigation system was repaired, and once again Mesopotamia became a center for world trade. Camel caravans moved slowly across the ancient Silk Road to China and the Far East, bringing grain, timber, and other products and returning with the gold, silver, fine silks, and precious stones sought by Mesopotamian merchants for their homes.

The Persian emperors were also tolerant of the customs, beliefs, and especially the religions of conquered peoples. Thus Cyrus allowed the Jews taken to Babylon in slavery by Nebuchadnezzar to return to their homeland.

Unfortunately the Persian empire lasted for barely two centuries, a short time by the long Mesopotamian standards. The empire was overextended territorially, and later rulers wasted much energy and fruitless effort in campaigns beyond its borders. Wars with the Greeks proved to be their biggest headache. In 333 B.C., Alexander, the king of Macedonia in northern Greece, defeated the Persian armies in several momentous battles and brought an end to the king's peace along with his empire. Due to its central location, Alexander (the Great, as history usually refers to him) made Babylon his capital. He led his army clear across Asia and into India to lay claim to a territory larger than the Persian empire. But on his return to Babylon, Alexander suddenly became ill and died, at the age of thirty-three. His generals divided up his newly conquered territories among themselves; one of them, Seleucus, received Mesopotamia as his share.

From then on, the land between the rivers became a battleground for foreign powers, establishing a pattern that exists to this day as Iran, Syria, Israel, and Iraq struggle to dominate the region. Some 2,000 years ago the names were different, as Persians, Romans, Greeks, and others fought with each other for control of the central Middle East, but the pattern established then endures.

As these divisive conflicts raged on, the once-great cities of Mesopotamia gradually sank into the earth. One knew their location only from the high mounds of earth (*tells*, in Arabic) that rise above the flat plain, the various layers of urban civilization buried far underground. Much earlier the biblical prophet Isaiah had predicted Babylon's fate: "It shall not be inhabited from generation to generation, nor shall shepherds make their flocks to lie down there, and wolves shall howl in the pleasant palaces." Similarly the prophet Nahum had forewarned the fate of the Assyrian capital: "Nineveh shall be laid waste; who shall bemoan her?"

Thus it must have seemed to the people living between the Tigris and Euphrates rivers and north to the Kurdish mountains in the seventh century A.D. that after thirty centuries their civilization had burnt itself out. Their future lay in the hands of outsiders, Persians and Romans in particular; their endless struggles had indeed laid waste the land.

But human history is marked by a constant process of decay and rebirth, like the earth which nourishes us. Unexpectedly a new force, sweeping northward from far south of the Mesopotamians in desert Arabia, revived their fortunes. The new force drew its power from religion, a religion new to the world although drawn from older roots. We call this religion Islam, and in the years to come it would reshape the lives of the people in the land between the rivers and make them a central part of a revitalized civilization.

CHAPTER TWO

WORLD CENTER FOR ISLAM

IN HIS EFFORTS to promote the dignity and self-respect of his people and pride in their nation, Saddam Hussein told them that "the glory of the Arabs stems from the glory of Iraq. Throughout history, whenever Iraq became mighty and flourished, so did the Arab nation. This is why we are striving to make Iraq mighty, formidable, able, and developed." Although the "Arab nation" as such exists only in Arab minds, his statement illustrates the mind-set of the Iraqi leader and his people. The "glory of the Arabs and of Iraq" reminds them of that period in history, roughly five centuries, when the land between the rivers was the center of a brilliant civilization. In its time, it was far superior to any civilization in Europe or the Americas; superior in technology, intellectual achievements, and discoveries in science, medicine, astronomy, mathematics, and other fields, which eventually reached the Western world in translated form. And it was a civilization founded on Islam, a new religion that emerged in Arabia in the seventh century A.D. and was

31

brought to the outside world by the Arabs, a people previously little known outside the Arabian Peninsula.

What is Islam? It is the third and youngest of the three great world religions that are monotheistic—that is, based on belief in One God rather than the numerous gods and goddesses that many ancient peoples believed would sometimes come to earth to influence human affairs. *Islam*, in the Arabic language, means "surrender" or "submission." Those who "submit" to God and obey His rules are known as Muslims. In this respect Islam is similar to Christianity and Judaism, the religion of the Jews. Where Muslims part company with Christians is over the divinity of Jesus. Muslims do not believe that God can be divided or take human form; He is indivisible and all-powerful. Muslims have great respect for Jesus and his teachings, and they believe he was one of a series of messengers (or prophets) who were inspired to bring God's Word to mankind and help people correct the evils in their lives and in the world. But they do not accept Jesus as the Son of God, sent into the world by God's decision and sustained by the Holy Spirit. In this respect Muslims are closer to Jews than to Christians, and their belief in One God as opposed to the Trinity has led to much conflict with Christians.

Another difference between Islam and Christianity is that Islam emerged in the full light of history through the experiences and teachings of a particular person, a man named *Muhammad* (the "Praised One" in Arabic). He lived in the remote city of Mecca, in southwestern Arabia, where he owned a caravan trading business. In those days the people of Mecca, and of Arabia in general, were polytheistic in their beliefs. That is, they believed in many gods and goddesses, most of whom were deities representing natural forces such as the sun and moon, rain, the winds, thunder, and lightning. The merchants of Mecca knew a good business deal when they saw one, and would charge substantial fees to pilgrims coming to Mecca to worship at the shrines of these various gods and goddesses.

Although Muhammad was unknown outside Mecca, he seems to have been highly respected in his hometown, not only for his business ability but also for his skills in mediating disagreements and settling disputes amicably. Around his city he was known as *al-Amin*, "the Just." But in his fortieth year this model citizen seems to have gone through a midlife crisis. Increasingly he felt dissatisfied with his own life and with the greed and selfishness he saw around him. He felt it was wrong for the merchants of Mecca to charge fees and make money from poor pilgrims who had come to worship at the shrines of the city.

Muhammad began leaving his home in the evenings and walking out into the country. Often he would climb up a nearby hill called Mount Hira and sit in a cave there for hours at a time, wrapped in a thin cloak to protect himself from the cold desert air. Then, during one of his vigils in A.D. 610, Muhammad heard a voice calling to him. It seemed to come from out of the dark sky. The voice said to him: "Recite!" Muslims believe that it was the voice of the Archangel Gabriel, the spokesman for God. As Muhammad described the experience, he replied: "I cannot." "Then the angel seized me," he continued, "and gripped my body till I could bear it no longer. Then he released me and said again: 'Recite!' Three times the angel seized me and gripped my body, and the third time he said: 'Recite in the name of your Lord who created, who created man from a clot of blood,' and I repeated it, my heart palpitating with terror." Thus it was that Muhammad knew that in some mysterious way he had received the Word of God, that he had been chosen as God's messenger to bring God's Word to the Arabs and through the Arabs to the whole world.[7]

What Muhammad received on that fateful night was apparently a revelation from God. It was to be the first of many he would receive during the short period of life, some twenty-two years, that remained to him. Muslims call that event the Night of Power, because it gave Muhammad the power to create a new religion based on belief in Allah, the God of the Arabs.

During the rest of his life Muhammad received a large number of revelations from God. These were given orally at first, but after his death, in A.D. 632, they were written down as the Koran (*Qur'an*, in Arabic), meaning "recitation." The Koran forms the basis of the faith of Islam. Muslims believe it is the literal Word of God, not the words of Muhammad, and although they revere him as prophet and messenger and seek to model their lives on his conduct and behavior, they do not worship him as divine.

In addition to belief in God, the Koran requires five actions of every Muslim. They are: (1) the confession of faith—"I say that there is no God but God, and that Muhammad is the Messenger of God; (2) prayer, five times daily at prescribed periods; (3) fasting for a full month during the daylight hours in Ramadan, the month of the Night of Power; (4) almsgiving or tithing, giving a fixed share of one's income for the support of the poor, the maintenance of mosques (Islamic houses of worship), and other community needs; and (5) pilgrimage at least once in one's lifetime to Mecca and Medina, cities associated with Muhammad's life and ministry. These five actions are usually called the Five Pillars because they "hold up" the "House" of Islam.

Other than his immediate family and a few close friends, very few people in Mecca joined the small Muslim community in its beginning stages, after the first revelations. The city's leading families even opposed Muhammad, partly because he criticized the mistreatment of the poor by wealthy merchants but also because he denounced the worship of many gods and goddesses that had made Mecca a center for pilgrimages and festivals in Arabia. As the opposition to his ministry increased, Muhammad and his followers began to fear for their lives. In 622, rumors of a plot to kill him caused the Muslims to flee. They were given refuge in another town, Medina, some 200 miles (320 kilometers) from Mecca. The leaders of Medina had been trying without success to settle a feud between clans that had caused much unnecessary bloodshed. Muhammad's reputation as an arbitrator led them to invite him to come and settle the feud. He did so, and in gratitude the entire population of Medina became Muslim, the first place in Arabia to become entirely Islamic. This event, called the Hegira (*Hijrah*, "emigration" in Arabic), marks the start of Islam as a formally organized religion. The year A.D. 622 became Year One of the Islamic calendar. Muhammad now had a power base from which to launch attacks on the forces of Mecca and work his way back to his hometown. His own warriors won several small-scale clashes with the Meccans and began to cut off the pilgrimage routes. After eight years of intermittent conflict, Mecca's leaders grew weary of the struggle. They accepted Muhammad's peace terms: Mecca would become an Islamic city under his leadership, and the shrines of gods and goddesses there would be destroyed. Upon his return Muhammad went about the city personally smashing these shrines. Henceforth, he declared, Mecca would be a center for pilgrimage to Allah the One God.

Muhammad's last years in Mecca were busy ones, as tribe after tribe from all of Arabia "submitted" to Islam. Unfortunately only two years remained to him. He died unexpectedly after a short illness (possibly pneumonia) in 632. In what would be his last sermon, he told his followers that he

*The reception of Muhammad in Medina marks the
beginning of the Islamic calendar.*

was the last of the Messengers; there would be no more revelations. He reminded them that they were a special community, united in faith, with the obligation to go out into the world and convert peoples everywhere to Islam.

Muhammad died before he could name a successor to carry on his work, and because he had said that he was the last Messenger, the grieving Muslims were faced with a difficult decision. In this emergency they fell back on age, seniority, and majority rule. They chose Abu Bakr, Muhammad's father-in-law and first convert, as the first *caliph* ("agent," "deputy," or "representative") of Muhammad, who himself was the agent of God. However, a minority of the Muslims argued that Muhammad had intended to name Ali, his closest male relative and husband to his daughter Fatima, as his successor, but could not do so because of his sudden death. The minority argued that Muhammad's wisdom and insight, but not his prophetic powers, would have been passed on to members of his immediate family. This majority-minority split would have important consequences for Islam in general and Iraq in particular in later years.

Under the leadership of Abu Bakr and his three immediate successors, Islam burst out of Arabia and spread across the world. It was a revolutionary movement, but it was driven by religious inspiration. Muslim armies, initially Arab but soon to include warriors from other parts of the world, challenged the Persian empire and the Eastern Roman (Byzantine) Christian empire based in Constantinople (modern Istanbul, Turkey). These two were the major powers of the period, but they had battled each other to exhaustion, mostly in conflict over the land between the rivers that lay between their territories. The Muslims defeated Persian and Byzantine armies with equal skill. Within a few years of Muhammad's death Islam controlled the formerly Christian lands of Egypt, Lebanon, Syria, Jordan, and Palestine.

One way to describe these early Muslims is that their confidence and enthusiasm were unbounded. They were "as full of freshness as the desert air," bringing a message of salvation to the world, moving in the path of Allah."[8] After they had driven back the Byzantine armies, they turned their attention to the Persians. In 637 they defeated the Persian royal army in the famous battle of Qadisiya (kah-DEE-see-yah), cited by Arab leaders down to Saddam Hussein as the great victory of the Arab nation over the non-Arab Iranians. With this victory and the death of the Persian king, all of his lands, including Mesopotamia, became part of the caliph's domain.

The land between the rivers now became a province of the caliphate. The Arabs brought it a new language and a new name, *al-Iraq* ("mudbank" in Arabic, a reference to the annual Tigris-Euphrates floods that had made the growing of food crops so successful there). The ancient irrigation system was repaired, and tribes from Arabia were encouraged to migrate there, not only to ensure a Muslim majority but also to reward them for their loyalty. The Islamic policy of tolerance toward religious communities that based their belief system on "sacred books"—Jews, Christians, and Zoroastrians, for example—allowed them to survive and prosper. They were exempted from military service and required only to pay a separate tax, a sort of poll tax, which placed them under the caliph's protection. These communities were called "Peoples of the Book," who were allowed to manage their internal affairs with their own religious authorities.

The long-term effect of this policy may be seen in the present population structure of Iraq. It is about 5 percent Christian, representing various denominations. The Jewish population, of ancient origins, was greatly reduced after the establishment of the State of Israel. The Armenian community, fairly wealthy and important, is also of great age. In fact the Armenian Church in Baghdad is so old that it is regarded as sacred by Muslims, who worship there periodically.

As mentioned earlier in this chapter, the first three caliphs were elected by majority rule, over the objections of a vocal minority. The third caliph, Uthman, a member of the Meccan elite who had originally opposed Muhammad, was murdered in 656, a victim of the tribal conflict that affected Islamic politics early on. This left Ali as the only logical candidate for the office. Since he had already been passed over three times, he was elected more or less by default as the fourth caliph.

The first four caliphs are referred to historically as "the Rightly Guided" due to their closeness to Muhammad and the "rightness" that enabled them to carry on his work. The majority of Muslims throughout the world accept them as legitimate leaders of the faith. They also believe in the course of Islamic history as it actually happened, down to the present. In their own lives they follow the *Sunna* ("Way"), the proper way of life ordained by God, revealed to Muhammad, and defined in the Koran. For these reasons they are known as Sunnis.

Since Ali had been elected as the fourth caliph, one would expect that his election would have resolved the majority-minority controversy. However, his former opponents challenged his fitness to hold the office. Conflict between the two groups, along with other factors, soon led to civil war within the House of Islam. Ali was murdered in 661, after he had attempted to arbitrate his dispute with his major rival, a cousin of the murdered third caliph, Uthman. His murderer said he had acted because the office of caliph should never be traded or made subject to arbitration.

Ali's rival now declared himself caliph, and the majority of Muslims accepted his leadership. But the struggle between majority and minority was not over yet. In 680, Ali's younger son Husayn, the Prophet's grandson, was persuaded by his supporters to declare himself the rightful successor to Ali as head of the House of Islam. Husayn had been living for safety reasons in Kufa, a town in Mesopotamia newly founded by the forces of Islam after they had defeated the Persians. Husayn set off from there with a small band of loyal horsemen intending to go to Damascus, capital of the Syrian province of the caliphate, to confront his rival. A much larger force intercepted Husayn and his group, who were surrounded and killed almost to the last man in the marshes near the present-day city of Karbala. Husayn's severed head was brought to Damascus as proof of his death.

Husayn's murder provided the Muslim minority with a ready-made martyr, one of the prerequisites for an organized group. They called themselves *Shi'at Ali* ("Party of Ali"), commonly known as Shias. The conflict that separated Sunnis and Shias politically has had important consequences for Iraq. The area had been a base of operations for Ali and Husayn, and their tombs in Karbala and the nearby city of Najaf became centers of pilgrimage for Shia Muslims second only to Mecca in importance, as they are to this day. Over the centuries, in fact, Iraq and its neighbor Iran have acquired a Shia majority in their populations, 95 percent in Iran and 55 percent in Iraq.

THE ABBASID CALIPHATE

By the middle of the eighth century A.D. the Islamic lands of the caliphate stretched in a narrow band from Morocco on the northwest Atlantic coast of Africa eastward to the borders of India, some 4,400 miles (7,040 kilometers) in length. Its north-south axis reached from Central Asia southward for 2,400 miles (3,840 kilometers) to the southern end of Arabia. Islamic territory included nine-tenths of Spain and Portugal in Europe. Muslim mission-

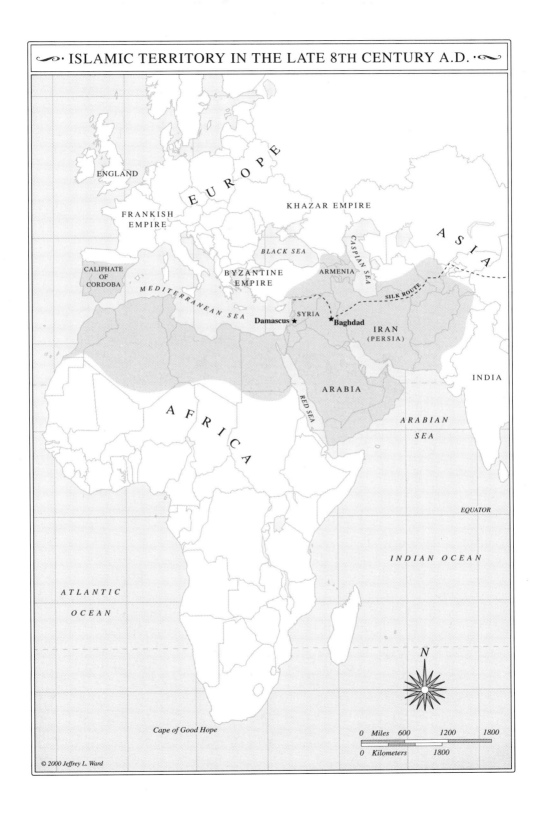

·ISLAMIC TERRITORY IN THE LATE 8TH CENTURY A.D.·

ENGLAND

E U R O P E

FRANKISH
EMPIRE

KHAZAR EMPIRE

A S I A

CALIPHATE
OF
CORDOBA

BLACK SEA

CASPIAN SEA

ARMENIA

M E D I T E R R A N E A N   S E A

BYZANTINE
EMPIRE

SILK ROUTE

Damascus ★   SYRIA   ★ Baghdad

IRAN
(PERSIA)

INDIA

RED SEA

ARABIA

A F R I C A

ARABIAN
SEA

EQUATOR

INDIAN OCEAN

ATLANTIC

OCEAN

N

Cape of Good Hope

| 0 | Miles | 600 | 1200 | 1800 |

| 0 | Kilometers | 1800 |

© 2000 Jeffrey L. Ward

aries carried the faith even farther afield, winning large numbers of converts in the East Indies (modern Indonesia), the Philippines, western China, and parts of Africa south of the Sahara Desert.

This vast territory was held together by the bond of Islam and obedience to the caliph, then ruling in Damascus. But the social and religious unity of Islam has never been matched by its political cohesiveness. A variety of political factors—the insistence of the Arabs on their superiority to other Muslims because of their founding role, tribal rivalries, and resentment of the luxurious lifestyle of the Damascus leadership—brought about a full-scale revolt. A new set of leaders seized power, calling themselves *Abbasids* after Muhammad's uncle Abbas.

Under the leadership of the Abbasid caliphs the Islamic world reached a level of civilization unmatched anywhere in the world. Its center was Iraq, and the hub and moving spirit of this brilliant civilization was the new city of Baghdad, founded and laid out by the caliph Al-Mansur on the west bank of the Tigris River in 762.

Baghdad was probably the world's first completely planned city. It was round, with an outer ring of huge walls and two concentric inner rings sheltering shops and buildings. In the city center was a large plaza that contained the great mosque, larger than any European cathedral, the green-domed palace of the caliph, and other royal residences. Four high gates provided entrance through arcades from the four directions. The building of Baghdad took more than four years and the efforts of 100,000 craftsmen, laborers, architects, and engineers. According to the chronicles, the caliph himself supervised construction, carrying bricks with his own hands.

Like its vanished predecessor, the Babylon of antiquity, Baghdad was almost literally the stuff of dreams. It was built as a river port, and shallow-draft boats traveled up the Tigris from the Persian Gulf and Indian Ocean

One of the restored gates to the city of Babylon.

bringing goods from the far-flung Islamic trading empire to the city's markets. In this way a network of trade linked the Mediterranean with China and India through Baghdad. Muslim writers called it the navel of the universe because of its wealth and central location. One of its names was *Medinat al-Salam* ("City of Peace"), and those fortunate enough to live there were transported at death from one paradise to another, according to an old proverb.

The Abbasid caliphs were also patrons of science, literature, and the decorative arts. Craftsmen from many places, not only Muslims but also artisans from Christian Italy and Greece, were hired to beautify mosques and palaces, as well as private homes, with delicate calligraphy. Promotion and patronage led to many important breakthroughs in science, mathematics, medicine, and astronomy, among other fields, at a time when Europe languished in the Dark Ages. Thus the caliphs' mathematicians gave us Arabic numerals and the concept of zero. Navigators owe a great debt to their Muslim counterparts who developed the sextant, octant, compass, and other essential navigation instruments. As for literature, it was said that by the end of the ninth century there were more than a hundred bookstores in the city of Baghdad alone!

One other significant contribution of Islamic civilization was the manufacture and use of paper. Papermaking was developed much earlier in China, and when a Muslim army invaded China and defeated Chinese forces they brought back several Chinese papermakers as prisoners. Their skill was soon discovered, and the caliph set them to work teaching papermaking skills to his own craftsmen. In time, the use of paper replaced that of the more cumbersome and less durable parchment in all official documents, not only in the Islamic lands but eventually through exchange in Europe as well.

THE MONGOL INVASION

The Abbasid caliphate lasted for five centuries, far longer than its predecessor and more than ten times that of the modern Iraqi state. But to describe it as united under the rule of the caliphs during that long period would be politically incorrect. Spiritually and morally the caliphs continued as heads of Islam. Politically, however, various centers of power developed, ruled by military commanders or adventurers loyal to the caliph but acting as heads of state in their respective territories. By the mid-eleventh century A.D. the caliph had become a figurehead; real power even in Baghdad was held by his personal army. And this army consisted almost entirely of Turks, warriors from Central Asia newly converted to Islam.

What followed has often been described as Iraq's and Islam's darkest period, the equivalent of the European

Dark Ages. In the mid-thirteenth century A.D. a horde of wild-riding horsemen appeared out of the East, sweeping across the lands of Islam in the same manner as the desert warriors who had first brought the new faith out of Arabia. The horsemen were Mongols, distant relatives of the Turks who had wandered for thousands of years across western China and eastern Central Asia in search of water and pasture for their flocks of sheep and goats. Traditionally, they were grouped into warring clans and tribes, often fighting over the same water and pastures. But somewhat unexpectedly a leader arose among them who united the clans and tribes under his control through bravery and force of personality. His name was Temujin, but the world remembers him as Genghis Khan.

With unity came movement, and Genghis Khan's Mongols headed west, more in search of empire, it seems, than of water and pasturage. They seemed unstoppable as they moved from city to city in the Islamic eastern lands, burning those that resisted and leaving huge piles of skulls to mark their passage. Today the descendants of these wild horsemen may be found in Iraq and neighboring countries where they live as peaceful farmers and herdsmen. It is hard to imagine the destruction created by their ancestors. Baghdad was besieged and captured in A.D. 1258. The last caliph was beheaded, the Mongol leaders charging him with corruption and disobedience to Islam, ironically quoting from the Koran to justify the action. The Mongols destroyed the irrigation system as part of their campaign to subdue Iraq, even deviating the courses of the Tigris and Euphrates rivers.

The date A.D. 1258 is often cited as marking the end of the Abbasid Caliphate and with it the collapse of Islam as a world power. But the history of Islam, like that of other similar movements, seems more accurately described as a series of ups and downs, periods of grandeur and retrenchment. For the land between the rivers, however, the Mongol invasion marked the end of its importance as the center for Islamic civilization. Henceforth until the twentieth century it would remain a backwater politically and economically, its destiny managed by outsiders.

CHAPTER THREE

A NATION EMERGES

THE DESTRUCTION of Baghdad and other Iraqi cities by the Mongols, followed by a later invasion of the Tartars, a Central Asian tribe related to the Turks and led by another would-be world conqueror, Tamerlane, left the once-brilliant Islamic civilization devastated. The irrigation system that had made agriculture successful and brought wealth to the land no longer functioned, due in part to damage by the invaders but also to lack of maintenance. Villagers fled from one place to another, often barely ahead of enemy forces, while the cities that had resisted the Mongols or Tartars were marked by towers of the skulls of their inhabitants. And with the death of the caliph, Islam no longer had a leader who combined spiritual with kingly authority.

A more serious effect economically was the discovery of the sea route around the Cape of Good Hope in extreme southern Africa by Portuguese navigators. This enabled the nations of Europe to trade more safely and easily with China, India, and the East Indies for their silks, spices, and other rare products unobtainable at home. The

47

new sea route also avoided the dangers of travel across the Middle East and Central Asia via the famous Silk Road to China. As a result Iraq became a political and economic backwater, a mudbank fought over by rival chiefs interested in power but not in the welfare of the people.

THE OTTOMAN EMPIRE

At this low point in the development of Iraq in particular and the Islamic world in general, a new force emerged out of the Middle East in one of the cycles of change that mark the history of Islam. A small tribe of Turks, migrating like many others from Central Asia into the lands of the former caliphate, were given a grant of land by a local ruler in Anatolia (modern Turkey) in return for their help in a conflict with his rivals. The tribe had no name, but its members referred to themselves as *Osmanlis*, "sons of Osman," from the name of their tribal chief. Their land grant was close to the border between Islamic territory and that of the Christian Byzantine empire based in Constantinople. Being warlike by nature and custom, the Osmanlis were readily converted to Islam and soon became the main support of Islam in its ongoing conflict with the Christians. They believed in the concept of the *ghazi*, the "fighter for the faith against the unbeliever." Like the modern suicide bomber, the ghazis felt it was their duty to defend and expand the lands of Islam and be willing to give their lives for the cause they believed in. Thus in death they would become martyrs to God and be taken directly to heaven.[9]

The new warriors for the faith took full advantage of their strategic location near the border between Christianity and Islam. They defeated the Byzantines in a number of clashes, and in A.D. 1326, Osman's son and successor, Orhan, captured the important Byzantine city of

Bursa. It became his new capital, and in rewarding himself for his services he took the title of Sultan and Commander of the Faithful following the usual custom of military leaders in the cause of Islam.

Thereafter the Ottomans, as they are usually known in history rather than the sons of Osman, expanded their conquests until they were the strongest power in the Islamic world. After establishing their rule over Anatolia, they crossed the narrow Bosphorus strait into Europe, and as a result were able to surround the Byzantine capital of Constantinople. On May 29, 1453, the army of Sultan Mehmet II captured the city, ending a thousand years of Christian domination in the Middle East in the name of Rome.

With Constantinople as their new power base, Ottoman armies pushed on into eastern Europe, adding Greece, Bulgaria, Albania, Hungary, Serbia, and part of Romania to their dominions. Their navy and its auxiliary force, the corsairs of North Africa, soon became the scourge of the Mediterranean. After the conquest of Egypt the Ottoman sultans added the title of caliph to a list that included Shadow of God on Earth, Lord of the Two Worlds, and Sovereign of the Seas. For the first time since the fall of the Abbasids, spiritual and temporal power in Islam was held by a single ruler.

IRAQ BETWEEN TWO EMPIRES

The Ottomans were Sunnis, members of the majority of Muslims. But as was noted in Chapter Two, Iraq was a very important place for Shia Muslims due to its associations with the caliph Ali and his murdered son Husayn.

Because the Shia have always been a minority in Islam, they express outwardly their obedience and allegiance to the head of state in the country where they live. In the past this was the caliph, or the sultan-caliph after the establishment of the Ottoman empire. But privately Shia focus their obedience on a line of *imams* as their true spiritual leaders. There were twelve imams in all, descendants of Ali through Husayn and his family. However, the twelfth Imam disappeared from his home in Samarra, Iraq, in A.D. 874. He was probably kidnapped and killed by agents of the caliph. But in order to keep the Shia community from falling apart due to the loss of its leader, the Shia religious scholars spread the word that he had not been killed but had been "taken up" by God and placed somewhere between heaven and earth, so that he is invisible to human eyes. He will return to earth at the proper time, they said, to announce the Day of Judgment and restore justice to the world. In Shia belief he is referred to as the *Mahdi*, the "Awaited One." Just as pious Jews await the coming of the Messiah and Christians the return of Jesus, the Shia wait for the return of the Mahdi to "set things right" for them and for the world of Islam.

The conflict over leadership between majority and minority in Islam reached a new level with the establishment of Ottoman control over much of the Islamic world and the emergence of a rival Shia power in Iran in the fifteenth century. It began in an Islamic religious order (somewhat similar to the orders of monks in Christianity) called the *Safavi* from the name of its founder. The founder was widely respected for his wisdom and his ability to heal the sick and perform other miracles. The order that he founded was known as the dervish, from the Persian word *darwish*, meaning "poor." Its members took a vow of poverty when they joined the order and devoted their lives to study and prayer. But the order itself became wealthy through the purchase of lands. Eventually its wealth attracted the attention of the Ottomans, and to protect itself it sought the support of a Turkish tribe living in northwestern Iran and northeastern Iraq. The Turkish tribe was Shia, and although the Safavi order was nominally Sunni, its members now joined the Shia tribes-men in opposition to the sultan.

As a result the relationship between Sunni Ottoman and Shia Iranian leaders turned from tolerance to outright conflict. The Safavis initially established their authority over the eastern part of the Middle East, including mud-bank Iraq, plus a large part of Central Asia. The Safavi leader then assumed the title of shah in keeping with Per-sian imperial tradition. His name was Ismail, and he was already a seasoned warrior at the age of twelve! Despite his death at a relatively young age, barely in his thirties, Shah Ismail played an extremely important role in the development of Iran as a separate Islamic state, along with that of Iranian-ruled Iraq. In 1501 he declared that hence-forth Twelver Shiism (belief in the Twelve Imams) would be the official state religion of Iran. He invited all Shia liv-ing outside the country to come there and be assured of protection from the Sunni majority. Sunnis living in Iran were ordered to become Shia or risk imprisonment.

Shah Ismail's declaration changed Iran forever. Even today it is the only Islamic state that is officially Shia, its spe-cial status defined as such in the constitution of the present-day Islamic republic. Iraq was then under Safavid control, and after the occupation of Baghdad the Sunni population was actively persecuted by the tribal allies of the Shah. Also, in eastern Turkey these tribesmen supported uprisings of the Shia population there, an action that drew a prompt response from the sultan. A huge Ottoman army, its num-bers swollen by a large contingent of horse-drawn artillery, marched into Iraq and routed the Safavid forces in 1514 at the battle of Chaldiran, an early example of the superiority of the new military technology over the cavalry and archers of traditional Middle Eastern forces.

Victory at Chaldiran gave the Ottomans control of Iraq, but thereafter the land between the rivers alternated between Ottoman and Safavid control, as a border province.

The area was formally incorporated into the Ottoman empire by treaty in the seventeenth century. The treaty was "arranged" by European diplomats, since treaties between sovereign states in the European sense of the term did not exist in the Islamic world.[10]

OBSTACLES TO NATION-BUILDING

The periodic Ottoman-Safavid wars and the Sunni-Shia differences responsible for these wars were hard on the people of Iraq. The Ottomans divided the land into three *vilayets* (provinces), each one named for its principal city (Baghdad, Basra, and Mosul). Each vilayet had a governor appointed by the sultan in Constantinople. However, these governors were not natives of the land and were interested only in making enough money from their posts to be able to retire comfortably to their summerhouses in the Princes Islands in the Sea of Marmara. Economic and social progress were nonexistent; by the mid-1600s the population of Baghdad had dwindled to 20,000.

A major difference among groups in the Iraqi population developed as a result of the struggle for control of the land by the Ottomans and the Safavids. While the Safavids were in control, many Shia moved there to put themselves under the shah's protection. Soon they formed a majority of the population. Shia representatives in Najaf and Karbala were appointed to look after the needs of Shia pilgrims to those cities. This arrangement continued after the Ottoman reconquest. However, the Ottoman authorities limited the stay of pilgrims to ten days, reasoning that if allowed to remain longer they would do so, thereby forming a potentially disloyal element in the population and perhaps joining the Iranians in the event of a renewal of war. In the same vein, other obstacles to nation-building developed out of the basic diversity of the Iraqi population (especially its Muslim and non-Muslim elements). During this period various large tribes from Arabia migrated northward and established themselves in particular areas, notably in the south and around Baghdad. In the northern Mosul vilayet powerful Kurdish clans controlled the mountainous area of Kurdistan. Due to their mountain location and fiercely independent spirit the Kurds were difficult to govern (as they still are), and the Ottomans found it easier to rule them indirectly through their tribal chiefs. The same principle was applied to the Arab tribes. As a result, Ottoman authority was limited to the cities, where Ottoman governors could depend upon the complaisance of the urban population.

THE TANZIMAT REFORMS

In the nineteenth century the Ottoman government undertook a series of reforms in administration and management. The reforms came as the result of European pressure. The Russians, expanding their land empire southward, had seized large sections of former Ottoman territory, and the British had helped subject peoples like the Greeks and Serbs to win their independence. The Ottoman empire had shrunk enormously from its earlier extent, and seemed to be ruled so ineffectively that European statesmen referred to the sultan as "the Sick Man of Europe."

At this critical stage in the survival of his empire, the sultan and his advisers decided on a bold policy, which they thought might help the "sick man" recover. They called the policy *Tanzimat*, a Turkish word meaning "reorganization." The policy was announced in two "imperial decrees." The first guaranteed the equality of all subjects of the empire, Muslim as well as non-Muslim, in such matters as taxation, military service, civil-service appointments, and access to state-supported higher education.

The Tanzimat reformers borrowed freely from European models, notably law codes and ministries, such as a ministry of education and a ministry of justice, to supervise the new legal system.

The Tanzimat decrees breathed new life into the stagnant air of Iraq. In 1869 a new governor arrived in Baghdad with the responsibility of implementing them. His name was Midhat Pasha, and he may be considered in many respects the founder of the modern Iraqi state. Midhat Pasha's goal was to make Iraq a model province of the empire. The areas of emphasis in his program were government, education, and land reform to break up the independent power of large landowners and the tribes. Education, to Midhat, was the key to social and economic progress. Thus he founded the first technical school and set up what we would call middle and high schools. Previously, Muslim children had been able to attend only the Islamic primary schools, where they were taught to memorize the Koran until they had it letter-perfect. A handful of young men (no girls) were able to study in the *madrasas*, religious schools that taught Islamic subjects such as theology and law. Midhat's new schools offered a European-style curriculum with such familiar subjects as mathematics, science, geography, and foreign languages. And the new schools were open to all and free of cost.

WORLD WAR I

World War I was crucial to the modern Middle East, the catalyst in the establishment of its modern nations. The Ottoman empire, unwisely, departed from the usual practice of its leaders in playing off the European powers in order to preserve what was left of its territories, and allied itself with Germany against Britain, France, and Russia. As a result Ottoman Iraq became one of the principal battle-

grounds of the Middle East. The British needed to control
it in order to protect the oilfields of neighboring Iran,
being developed by a British company, and to guard
British sea routes through the Persian Gulf and Indian
Ocean to India. A British invasion force landed at Basra in
1914 and headed for Baghdad, expecting little opposition.
It outran its supply lines, however, and was trapped in the
Iraqi city of Kut and forced to surrender after a long siege
by Ottoman forces. It was not until 1918, after the
Ottoman government signed an agreement with its oppo-
nents, that the British were able to occupy all of Iraq.

THE ARABS: A HOUSE DIVIDED

The Ottoman defeat was not unexpected given the poor
health of the Sick Man of Europe, and while the war was
going on France and Britain made secret agreements to
divide up the remaining Ottoman territories and rule
them as colonies. These agreements involved the empire's
Arab territories, those populated mainly by Arabs. The
most important one was the Sykes-Picot Agreement,
named after the two diplomats who negotiated it. It gave
the area of modern Syria and Lebanon to France, with the
British controlling Iraq and Transjordan (modern Jordan).
Palestine (modern Israel) would be managed by an international government in view of its special religious status.

While this agreement was being negotiated a group of
British agents based in Cairo, Egypt, were negotiating
with Arab leaders to urge them to revolt against the
Ottomans. In return for their help, the British agents
"promised" an independent Arab state composed of Syria,
Lebanon, Iraq, Transjordan, and Palestine. A huge amount
of controversy has resulted over what was promised to
the Arab leaders. The only evidence that exists is an
exchange of ten letters between the British high commis-

sioner to Egypt, Sir Henry McMahon, and Husayn, the sharif of Mecca, guardian of the Islamic Holy Places and the ranking Arab leader in the Ottoman empire. But on the basis of the correspondence Sharif Husayn called for an Arab revolt in 1916. He denounced the sultan as an enemy of Islam, and an Arab tribal force led by the Arabic-speaking T. E. Lawrence (author of the desert classic *The Seven Pillars of Wisdom*) and the sharif's son Faisal (who would later become ruler of Iraq) defeated the Ottomans in several engagements. In 1918 it joined regular British forces to ride in triumph into Damascus.

The previously mentioned secret agreements, plus another arranged by the British with Jewish leaders to establish a Jewish national home in Palestine, became public knowledge after the war, when Allied leaders met to work out the terms of a peace treaty with defeated Germany and the Ottoman empire. The resulting treaty, which was signed reluctantly by the sultan, was a bitter blow to Arab leaders. Instead of the independent Arab state they thought they had been promised, they found themselves ruled by new masters. The only sugar-coating allowed was that the colonies were officially described as "mandates." The term was developed by the newly formed League of Nations, and it obligated the mandate powers (Britain and France) to train their subject peoples for eventual independence and report progress toward this goal in annual reports to the League.

THE BRITISH MANDATE

The period of the British mandate (1920–1932) was critical to the formation of Iraq as an independent nation. Its prospects in the beginning, however, were not promising. Basra was separated from Baghdad by vast unnavigable marshes, the home of descendants of the ancient Sumerians, and dwellers in reed huts hidden away from public view. The Mosul area was the home of the Kurds, non-Arab Sunni Muslims with a language and culture different from those of the Arab majority. Depending on where they lived, the Iraqis traditionally looked to the tribal sheikh, village headman, or religious leader for guidance and protection

Other social divisions separated Sunnis from Shia, city dwellers from villagers, rich landowners and merchants from rural peasants, and mountaineers from lowlanders, making Iraq, as one observer noted, "a difficult land to govern or develop."[11] Proof of this was forthcoming after the arrival of British administrators. A tribal revolt broke out in 1920, and for several months the British lost control. Eventually they were forced to bring in heavy tanks and artillery to crush the revolt, and the cost was high—four hundred British lives and millions of pounds. Like the long-ago battle of Qadisiya (see Chapter One), the 1920 revolt is viewed by the present-day Iraqi regime as a genuine nationalist uprising, one that brought the various sections of Iraqi society together in a common struggle against foreign occupation. As such it may be considered a first step in the emergence of an Iraqi nation.

The next chapter will examine the process whereby Britain shaped this nation. It began as indirect rule, with British advisers governing through an elected king (who was not a native Iraqi). Iraq was the first country ruled under League of Nations mandate to be granted formal independence, and in that sense the British could say, with some justification, that they had discharged their obligations to the League and had kept their promise to the people of Iraq.

CHAPTER FOUR

FROM MONARCHY TO REVOLUTION

IN 1921 the Forty Thieves, as Winston Churchill called them, met in Cairo, Egypt, to map out Iraq's future as a nation to be trained for self-government under British control as a League of Nations mandate. Churchill, newly appointed secretary of state for colonies, was at the beginning of his distinguished career and seems not to have been much interested in the meetings. He spent most of his time making sketches of the Pyramids. But the Forty Thieves took their responsibilities seriously. They agreed that Iraq should begin its national life as a monarchy on the British model, with a constitution, parliament, and other institutions of democratic government. The country would need a king who would be acceptable to the many different factions and groups in the population. He would also have to be an outsider, since no native Iraqi leader was capable of uniting the people and building an Iraqi nation. It seemed to be a difficult task to find the right ruler for the new country.

However, the right kind of ruler just happened to be available—Faisal, son of the sharif of Mecca and leader of

Arab forces in the revolt against the Ottomans (see Chapter Three). After Faisal had entered Damascus in triumph in 1918, Arab leaders proclaimed him king of Syria, the new Arab kingdom uniting the Arabs of Syria, Lebanon, Transjordan, Palestine, and Iraq in an independent state. The new state would fulfill the "pledges" made by the British in the Husayn-McMahon correspondence to help the Arabs gain self-rule. Britain, however, had no intention of honoring its supposed pledge. Instead, Britain and France proceeded to divide up the Arab lands of the Ottoman empire according to the terms of the Sykes-Picot Agreement. The agreement gave Iraq, Transjordan, and Palestine to Britain as mandates; France would receive Syria and Lebanon as its share of the territories. The British had already occupied Iraq. Now the French sent Faisal an ultimatum: abdicate or accept French rule. When he refused, French tanks and artillery bombarded Damascus, putting a quick end to Arab dreams of independence. It would be a quarter-century before Syria and Lebanon were free from foreign control, and meanwhile Faisal was out of a job, throneless and adrift in Middle Eastern sands.

It seemed to the Forty Thieves that Faisal might be a suitable candidate for the vacant and nonexistent throne of Iraq. As an outsider he was not identified with any of the Iraqi population groups that had always made the country difficult to govern. Owing to his family's descent from the Prophet Muhammad and his father's position in the Islamic world as Guardian of the Holy Places, he held the respect of both Sunnis and Shias. Also, he had fought with the British in the Arab Revolt and had demonstrated military skills. Lawrence of Arabia, one of the Forty Thieves and Faisal's comrade in arms, urged the others to approve him as king, while Gertrude Bell, the only female member, assured them that the Iraqi tribal leaders who had been her companions on many desert journeys would be pleased to have him as their ruler. Bell even drew lines

on the Egyptian sands to sketch out what she felt were
the correct boundaries of the new kingdom.

In 1921, Faisal arrived in Baghdad to take charge of Iraq's destiny. Several thousand British, Arab, and tribal dignitaries gathered in the courtyard of a former Ottoman palace to greet him, while a military band played "God Save the King" and Gertrude Bell watched from the front row. For her efforts on Faisal's behalf she had become known as the uncrowned queen of Iraq, and for some years thereafter she continued to play that role as the king's personal adviser.[12]

THE MANDATE, 1921–1932

A treaty in 1922 between Britain and Faisal's government defined Iraq as a constitutional monarchy with a constitution as the "law of the land." The constitution also established a national legislature (parliament), with political parties, free elections, and a free press. The government itself would be managed by a cabinet of ministries similar to the U.S. and British cabinets, with ministers appointed by the king. Annexes to the constitution would protect the rights of foreigners working in Iraq to develop the country as well as the rights of religious and ethnic minorities.

These features of the political systems of the Western world were almost unknown to most Iraqis. The 1920 revolt had foreshadowed their anger at being occupied and controlled by a foreign Christian country, and their ongoing resentment made the development of self-government difficult. But the British were less interested in bringing democracy to Iraq than in installing an Iraqi government that would guarantee British control and safeguard long-term British economic and strategic interests. A British official served as the real boss of every government department, looking over the shoulder of his Iraqi counterpart to make sure that he did what was best for Britain. The British also controlled Iraq's defense through a network of air bases spread throughout the country. British officers organized and trained Iraq's new national army, and a British High Commissioner not only looked after Britain's interests but also was the final authority over the king in matters of foreign policy and the development of the Iraqi state.

Iraq's boundaries were not fixed until 1926, when the northern largely Kurdish-populated province of Mosul was included in its territory. The province had been occupied by British forces after the 1918 armistice that ended World War I, and the new government of the Turkish Republic, successor to the Ottoman empire, claimed that the British occupation was illegal under international law. Britain and Turkey then asked the League of Nations to mediate their dispute over Mosul. The International Court of Justice (World Court), an agency of the League concerned with questions of international law, awarded Mosul to Iraq, noting that the province had never been separated from Iraqi territory and that its population was different from the Turks. As a result Britain gained legal control over the important oil resources of northern Iraq, which were already being developed by a British oil company.

As the nucleus for his new government, Faisal depended upon a group of young men known as the Sharifians, from their association with his father the sharif of Mecca. In fact they were all native Iraqis, Sunni Muslims from Baghdad who had served in the Ottoman army but had taken part in the Arab Revolt. They not only were trained in military matters but also better educated than the majority of the population. Both Faisal and his British advisers found it useful to work with the Sharifians rather than include representatives of other Iraqi groups such as the Shia, the Kurds, and other non-Arabs. Under this arrangement Iraq's government is best described as a "triangle of power," with the British at one corner, the king at another, and the Sharifians forming a third corner. This sharing of power, however, effectively excluded the majority of Iraqis from taking any part in the building of their new nation.

Despite being an outsider, King Faisal soon became a unifying symbol for the new nation. He remained above the political conflicts of the various groups, and maintained good relations with the British. His special accomplishment aside from bringing political stability to the population lay in the creation of a national army. In view of the general anger over the British occupation and mandate and constant reminders of the destruction of the independent, united Arab kingdom of Syria, a national army would help to unite Iraqis and break down the walls of distrust between various groups.[13]

King Faisal I. This photo was taken in 1933, while he was on a visit to London.

In June 1930, Iraq signed a new treaty with Britain to end the mandate. Iraq would become an independent nation, ruling over its own territory. The British also sponsored Iraq's membership in the League of Nations. The country became a member of the League in 1932, the first to become independent and be given international recognition by other countries through the mandate process.

Independence, however, had strings attached to it—British strings. Britain kept the right to use its bases and Iraqi roads, airports, and harbors in the event of war, and to station troops and aircraft at those bases. Iraq was also required to "consult" with Britain on all matters of foreign policy. These strings brought a bitter commentary from an Iraqi poet:

> "In the Book of Politics we are a people
> Owners of Sovereignty, yet we do
> not even possess wreckage we could call our own.
> In the Book of Politics we are Free,
> Yet we are no more than handicapped orphans."[14]

The poet's words of protest echoed throughout the country in strikes and demonstrations. A manifesto circulated in Baghdad by members of an opposition political party said that the treaty was an insult to free Iraqis, and that the Iraqi parliament, which had ratified it, did not represent the people. But dominated as it was by Sunnis, progovernment representatives, and tribal chiefs, parliament quickly and almost unanimously approved it. Whether Iraq was ready for self-government after barely twelve years under British guidance was debatable. Just before his death, King Faisal noted sadly: "In Iraq there is still no Iraqi people but imaginable masses of human

beings, lacking any patriotic ideal, connected by no common tie, prone to anarchy and always ready to rise against
any government whatsoever."[15]

PROBLEMS AT HOME

In September 1933, King Faisal died under somewhat
mysterious circumstances while on a medical visit to
Switzerland. He left behind him a gap in leadership. His
son, Crown Prince Ghazi, lacked Faisal's steady hand and
ability to work with both the British and the various factions or groups in Iraqi society. Ghazi had been educated
in England and at the British-sponsored Military Academy
in Baghdad. But he was young (barely twenty-one), had
little or no experience in the government, and was more
interested in racing cars and other hobbies than in carrying on his father's work. The British ambassador to Iraq at
that time described him as "weak and unstable as water,
impossible to control, difficult to influence and dangerous
to all, especially to himself."[16] The evaluation proved only
too accurate when Ghazi was killed in a crash of his high-
powered sports car outside Baghdad. His son succeeded
him under the terms of the constitution as Faisal II, but
since he was only four years old, the late king's uncle
Abdul-Ilah was appointed regent.

As mentioned earlier in this chapter, Faisal I had been
responsible, with British help, for forming the Iraqi
national army. By the mid-1930s it had become deeply
involved in politics, as a rival power center to the Sharifian elite that ran the government. In 1933 the army had
crushed an uprising of the Assyrians, and this success
greatly enhanced army prestige.

This success, along with the suppression of several
tribal revolts, encouraged army leaders to seize power and

The Assyrians involved in the uprising of 1933 were a relatively peaceful Christian sect that had lived for centuries under Ottoman protection in eastern Turkey. During World War I they had sided with the British and French against their protectors, and as a result they were forced to leave their homeland. The British helped resettle most of them in Iraq, and in return for their loyalty Assyrians were recruited and assigned as guards at British military and air bases. "With their slouch hats and red and white hackles the swaggering Assyrians became the symbol of British domination of Iraq," wrote one scholar.[17] In 1933 they began to demand self-government for their territory, as a prelude to complete independence. This led to military action; army commanders ordered the massacre of all the residents of one village as an object lesson to the Assyrian population, and the "revolt" ended as quickly as it had begun.

overthrow the civilian government. In 1936, General Bakr Sidqi, the commander during the Assyrian campaign, seized control of the country and ordered the king to accept a military regime. This 1936 coup set the pattern for internal politics for the next four decades, ending only when the civilian Ba'th party now led by Saddam Hussein took complete control of the country. During those decades army commanders worked behind the scenes, vetoing or canceling any actions taken by the government or parliament that seemed to threaten the army's privileged position. But the army was also divided into factions. Bakr Sidqi himself was assassinated by one of his own men in 1937. Feuds and disagreements between army leaders and the civilian elite, within the elite, and elsewhere emphasized how difficult Iraq was to govern. Between

1937 and 1941 six military coups were attempted, and "forty-seven cabinets were formed and fell apart during those years, because of internal quarrels and not the lack of public or parliamentary support."[18]

The small size of the Sharifian elite also hampered nation-building. The elite was most like an exclusive club than a representative government. Nuri al-Said, who served as prime minister fourteen times between 1930 and 1958 and was Iraq's best-known leader in the outside world, was often fond of comparing his colleagues to a pack of playing cards. If you shuffle them often enough, he said, the same faces will turn up.

WAR WITH BRITAIN, 1941

World War II had been going on for two years by 1941, and Britain stood almost alone against the armies of Germany and its allies. German forces were well on their way to capturing Egypt, the main British base in the Middle East, and Iraq lay not far ahead. Some Iraqi army leaders were convinced that Germany would win the war. The situation seemed right for a coup that would rid Iraq of its British occupiers and the pro-British civilian government of Nuri al-Said at the same time. Army commanders forced Nuri to resign. They installed a civilian government led by Rashid Ali, a Baghdad lawyer, who had no military background and presumably would be controlled by the military. Rashid Ali and his military backers made contact with German agents who forwarded to the German government a request for arms and support with which they would drive the British from Iraq.

However, the anticipated weapons never arrived. The British transferred troops from India to reinforce their Iraqi garrisons and protect the vital oil pipeline from Kirkuk in northern Iraq to neutral Turkey. The Iraqi army commanders proved to be better politicians than military leaders, and their forces were quickly defeated. British forces captured Baghdad after barely a month, reestablishing the government of Nuri al-Said as Rashid Ali and his supporters fled the country.

FOREIGN AFFAIRS: THE PALESTINE PROBLEM

For the rest of World War II and on into the 1950s it was "politics as usual" in Iraq. Rashid Ali escaped to Germany and eventually found his way to Saudi Arabia, where he was given refuge by the Saudi royal family, rivals of Faisal's family for centuries. Other leaders of the coup eventually were returned to Iraq and hanged as traitors to the country. "Politics as usual" meant the constant shuffling of cards, with the same faces in government. Between 1946 and 1958 twenty-two different cabinets were formed. A new treaty, the Treaty of Portsmouth, was signed with Britain in 1948. The only limitations on Iraqi independence was the requirement that the country "consult" with Britain on defense matters.

However, events elsewhere in the Middle East had a bad effect on Iraq, just as the country celebrated full independence. The most serious event, for Iraqi Arabs, was the establishment of the State of Israel in 1948 in Palestine. That former Ottoman territory had become a British mandate after World War I, but Britain's efforts to train its largely Arab population for eventual self-government were hampered by a British wartime commitment to help the displaced Jews of the world to establish a homeland there. During the 1920s and 1930s, Jewish immigration and Palestinian Arab population growth produced two separate communities with different languages, religions, cultures, and historical experiences living in the same land and mutually hostile.

After World War II the British came under international pressure to help the Jewish survivors of Adolf Hitler's genocide, the extermination of the Jewish people in Europe, in their efforts to reach Palestine and establish a homeland there. The British were also under pressure from the newly independent Arab countries of the Middle East to establish Palestine as an independent Arab nation, one of their own and located in sovereign Arab territory. In 1948 the British decided they had had enough; they could not reconcile Palestinian Arab claims with Jewish claims. They said they would end their mandate over Palestine and transfer the "Palestine problem" to the United Nations (the international organization that had replaced the League of Nations after World War II). The UN would have to decide what was best for that troubled land. Should it be an Arab state with a Jewish minority, a Jewish state with an Arab minority, or two separate states, one Arab, one Jewish, with some type of government in common and some sort of international status for the holy city of Jerusalem, its capital?

The question of Palestine was one of the first international issues to be considered by the UN. The organization was brand-new, and the representatives of its member states had little experience in dealing with such thorny issues. They formed a Special Committee on Palestine (UNSCOP) to examine the issue. Since Iraq had been a founding member of the UN, an Iraqi delegation took part in the UNSCOP debates. The head of the delegation was Dr. Fadhel Jamali, educated at Columbia University. In later years he would become one of Iraq's best-known leaders, respected in his home country and abroad for his ability to straddle two cultures, Arab and European-American. But he was above all an articulate defender of the Palestine Arab cause, arguing that the Palestinian people should have the same right to control their own territory as other peoples control theirs. "Palestine," he said, "is a vital part of the Arab world, while Zionism [the organized movement to establish a Jewish state in Palestine] is poisoning the atmosphere between Jews and non-Jews there. It endangers peace and harmony everywhere. Nothing can remedy the situation except a return to the fundamental principles of the UN Charter. An independent Palestine along democratic lines where all rightful citizens enjoy equal rights and take part in the government is all that is needed."[19]

Jamali's recommendations were ignored. In 1947, UNSCOP submitted two proposals to the UN General Assembly, one from the majority on the committee, the

Members of the Arab League go into a huddle at a meeting of the UN General Assembly. The debate about the fate of Palestine was long and bitter.

other a minority report. The majority report proposed partition of Palestine into two separate states, one Jewish and one Arab; Jerusalem would become an international city under UN control. The minority report recommended partition into two states but with a common government, using the system of cantons in Switzerland as a model. The General Assembly voted to approve the majority report, and six months later, on May 14, 1948, the last British troops left Palestine as Jewish leaders proclaimed the establishment of the State of Israel.

COUNTDOWN TO REVOLUTION

The creation of Israel in the Arab heartland was and continues to be resented by most Arabs. The Iraqi army joined other Arab armies and Palestinian Arab irregular forces in an attempt to destroy the new Israeli state but were defeated and driven out of Palestine, a defeat vividly described in Arabic as *al-Nakba*, "the catastrophe." The Iraqi army in particular was poorly equipped and still had not recovered from its 1941 defeat by British forces. An armistice arranged by the UN in 1949 halted the fighting, but left the Israelis in control of their new state, surrounded by hostile Arab countries that would fight five more unsuccessful wars in their attempt to "drive the Jews into the sea," as Arab newspapers described the Arab goal.

The Arab failure in Palestine was one of a number of factors that led to the unexpected overthrow of the Iraqi monarchy in 1958. A second factor was the increasingly pro-British policy of Nuri al-Said's government. Nuri had come to dominate Iraqi politics after the overthrow of Rashid Ali and his army associates. In 1956, Iraq joined with Britain, the United States, Pakistan, and Iran in the Baghdad Pact, a regional defense organization. The action led to much unrest in the country, with frequent strikes and demonstrations. The government imposed martial law and arrested several hundred people as a result.

Meanwhile a number of younger army officers had begun to meet secretly to plan the overthrow not only of Nuri al-Said's government but also of the monarchy. They were mostly from lower-class backgrounds; the two principal leaders, Brigadier Abdel Karim Qassem and Colonel Abdel Salam 'Arif, were sons respectively of a carpenter and a tailor. They called themselves the Free Officers, taking as their model the Free Officers in Egypt that had overthrown the monarchy there in 1952.

Opportunity knocked for the plotters in July 1958. The Iraqi government had just reached an agreement with Jordan for a union of the two Arab neighbors, and Iraqi army units had been ordered to Lebanon to help its government against an uprising there. As these units headed for Lebanon, 'Arif and Qassem convinced them instead to march on Baghdad and put an end to Nuri al-Said's plan to attach Iraq more closely to Britain. On July 14, 1958—ironically the anniversary of the 1789 French Revolution, which overthrew the king of France—soldiers seized the royal palace in Baghdad and killed the regent, the young king, and all but one member of the royal family. Mobs ransacked and burned the British embassy, while others hunted down officials of the former government. (Nuri al-Said escaped briefly, disguised in the black full-length robe of a peasant woman, but was discovered and killed several days later.) With his death and that of the regent, the king, and the Sharifian leadership, Iraq had turned a corner and entered a new life as a revolutionary military republic.

CHAPTER FIVE

TOWARD THE ONE-PARTY STATE

**IN CONTRAST** to the arrival of King Faisal in Baghdad seventeen years earlier, when Iraq's new ruler was greeted with sullen silence by the people, the July 14 revolution brought a wave of popular enthusiasm. Brigadier Abdel Karim Qassem, speaking on Baghdad Radio, declared that "all classes of the people have merged; there will be social justice and a higher standard of living for all." The co-leader of the Free Officers announced that "the army has liberated the corrupt crew that was installed by imperialism" (that is, Britain). With Nuri al-Said's violent death the House of Cards collapsed. Some members escaped; others were captured and given life sentences by a military court. "The age of feudal lords who crushed the people and foreigners who exploited them is now over," Qassem declared. "A new start is under way, and the past is to be forgotten."[20]

For starters the military leaders ordered the monarchy to be abolished. The old elite-dominated parliament was also closed down, and a new temporary constitution was approved that would declare Iraq a republic. The consti-

73

tution stated that Iraq was part of the "Arab nation" and that Islam was the official religion of the state.

Iraq's new leaders showed relative moderation in their treatment of former government officials, although probably motivated more by a desire to improve the country's image abroad than by revenge. After the initial bloodbath several of their death sentences were changed to prison terms, while others, notably Fadhel Jamali, were ultimately pardoned.

A significant change after the revolution was in foreign policy. Prior to 1958 this policy had been staunchly pro-Western. As noted in Chapter Four, Iraq had joined the U.S.-sponsored Baghdad Pact, and the army was almost completely dependent upon Britain for its weapons and equipment. Now Iraq turned leftward, toward the Soviet Union and its allies. Diplomatic relations were established with these countries, and Soviet arms began flowing into the land between the rivers to replace the outmoded British tanks, planes, and other weapons of war of the Iraqi armed forces.

At home, however, there was much less progress toward the establishment of a workable democratic political system. Although the majority of the people had supported the revolution, in practice the various social, political, and religious groups that had always made Iraq a difficult land to govern resumed their ancient power struggle. The difference was that the old elite had been able to keep this struggle under control, but now there was no center of power. Qassem, 'Arif, and their fellow Free Officers were little known outside the army, and they lacked a solid base of support.

Nor was there unity among the military leaders. Qassem and 'Arif had different, and opposing, visions of the future of the country. 'Arif admired Egypt's president Gamal Abdel Nasser, who had led a similar revolution in 1952. Nasser's goal was a strong, unified Arab nation, and as a first step toward that goal Egypt and Syria had just joined in the United Arab Republic (UAR). 'Arif believed the next step was for Iraq to join this union. Qassem's goal, in contrast, was to develop Iraq as a strong, free nation, one in which development of its vast resources for the benefit of its people would make the country a model for other developing nations in Asia and Africa. He felt that membership in the UAR would make Iraq a sort of junior partner, developing its resources for the benefit of others.

The Qassem-'Arif contest for power mirrored the larger problem of internal conflict among groups. A simple way to describe this conflict is in terms of Arab nationalists versus Iraqi patriots. Adding to the confusion was the large and well-organized Iraq Communist party (ICP), whose long-term goal was the establishment of Iraq as a socialist state. Qassem found the ICP a valuable ally in his struggle with 'Arif. After gradually outmaneuvering his rival, he had 'Arif arrested and charged with treason—attempting to establish a military dictatorship and overthrow the government. This pattern would continue to mark Iraqi politics until Saddam Hussein gained complete power in the 1970s. As one writer described it, "The political instability of revolutionary governments and the cycle of coups that became their trademark can be traced to this early struggle."[21]

THE "BLESSED LEADER" TAKES CHARGE

As the sole leader of the nation, Qassem was now "blessed," a term traditionally applied to those presumably given authority by God to direct the affairs of a particular Muslim group. Previously he had been almost unknown outside the army, but now his face, with its high forehead, thick black eyebrows, craggy jaw, and full head of dark hair, became a familiar sight on billboards and posters in public places. He was more a practical mind than a charismatic leader (one who could sway the masses

General Qassem reviews troops during a parade
marking the first anniversary of the Iraqi revolt.

with his speeches), and as a result he devoted his efforts
to matters such as a higher standard of living, education,
public housing, and land reforms at the expense of foreign
policy or interference with Iraq's neighbors. Although his
time in power was brief, many of the changes he intro-
duced formed the basis for Iraq's later development

LAND REFORM

Land reform, the redistribution of farmlands from rich to
poor farmers and those who had no land at all, was probably Qassem's major contribution to Iraq's development.

Prior to the revolution most of the country's agricultural land was owned by a small group of landowners, members of the elite and tribal sheikhs (chiefs). In the 1950s this group owned 90 percent of the total 8 million hectares (19.8 million acres) of farmland. In contrast, 85 percent of the farmers owned one hectare (2.5 acres) or less—the amount of land needed to support a family. This vast difference in ownership was made much worse by the fact that some 1.5 million sharecroppers and day laborers on farms owned no land at all.

Under these difficult circumstances the need for land reform was a priority. "It would destroy feudalism, the rule of the few over the many, and it would bring government benefits directly to rural people," observed one writer.[22]

Thus, on September 30, 1958, Qassem issued Law 30, the Agrarian Reform Law, that would lay the basis for redistribution of agricultural lands. No individual or family could own more than 250 hectares (618 acres) of irrigated land or 445 hectares (1,100 acres) of dry land (watered only by rainfall). Lands above these limits would be taken over by the government and distributed to small landowners and landless peasants. The law had a number of loopholes and weaknesses, and in the long run it was ineffective in closing the gap between rich and poor landowners. But it did have the positive effect of developing a solid base of support for Qassem among the rural population.

OIL

Oil, in the form of crude petroleum deposits, has been a visible feature of the land between the rivers for thousands of years. Wandering Bedouin (nomadic) tribes like that of the biblical patriarch Abraham did their cooking and lit their watch fires at night from the pools of thick black liquid seeping out of rocks in the desert or upland in the mountains of northern Mesopotamia. But the use of oil as a commercial fuel dates from only the early twentieth century. At that time the nations of Europe were competing for overseas trade and preparing for war. Oil would enable their ships, trains, airplanes, and other forms of transportation to travel faster and more economically than they could using coal or wood. Oil had been discovered in Iran in 1908, and geological surveys indicated the presence of similar deposits in northern Iraq.

As was noted in Chapter Four, control of these deposits was the main reason for the British occupation of Mosul province in 1918 and its inclusion in Iraq after the war.

During the British period the Iraqi oil industry was developed and managed by the British-owned Iraq Petroleum Company (IPC). Oil exports began in 1934, through a pipeline from the oilfield near Kirkuk to the ports of Haifa (in Palestine) and Tripoli (in Lebanon). However, IPC policy was to keep Iraqi oil production at a lower level than that of British and other European countries operating elsewhere in the Middle East. Thus Iraq's oil production in the 1940s averaged 140,000 barrels per day (bpd), while in Kuwait production was 350,000 bpd. This IPC policy was one of several issues that led to a permanently tense relationship with the state for the company.

These issues came to a head after the 1958 revolution. Other oil companies in the Middle East had agreed to a 50/50 split in royalties (payments made for oil sales abroad) with their respective host governments. The IPC, reluctantly, accepted this arrangement, and as a result Iraq's oil revenues shot up drastically. By 1961 they were $266 million, more than double 1953 totals. A number of new fields were discovered and brought into production, not only in the north but also in the central and southern areas of the country. Income from oil exports provided 90 percent of Iraq's foreign exchange (the amount in U.S. dollars and other foreign currencies paid as royalties).

Despite this windfall for Iraq, IPC still had complete control of the oil industry. The company set prices for its oil, made all decisions in regard to production and exports, kept 50 percent of profits, and controlled the entire concession area, the territory originally granted to it by the monarchy for future oil development.

In 1961, therefore, Qassem approved Public Law 80. It would cancel all but a small part of the original concession, leaving IPC in control only of those fields that were already in production. In this respect Qassem was ahead of his time. It would not be until the early 1970s that another oil-producing country, Libya, nationalized (gained complete control over) its oil industry. In Iraq's case the battle with IPC would continue for more than a decade, until the Blessed Leader's successors completed the job and the government-owned National Iraq Oil Company (NIOC) took control of the country's most important resource.

SOCIAL REFORMS

Qassem also initiated a number of important changes in the lives of his people. He had been a public-school teacher before entering the army, and educational improvements were a priority in his vision of the new Iraq. Hundreds of primary and secondary schools were built and thousands more young Iraqis enrolled in them. Youngsters walked for miles from their villages to the new schools if none happened to be nearby, such was their desire for education. There was a similar increase in the literacy rate, as thousands of adults flocked to the new schools to learn to read and write.

The new regime also invested much of its oil income in low-cost housing projects. The country's industrial development after World War II, with chemical plants, steel mills, oil refineries, and other factories springing up around the cities, encouraged many rural peasants to migrate to the cities in search of jobs and a better life. Most of these villagers arrived with little more than the clothes on their backs. The only housing they could afford—or even find—were *sarifas*, mud-brick shanties thrown up mostly overnight like a blanket of slums around Baghdad, Basra, and other cities. Qassem ordered the *sarifas* of Baghdad bulldozed to the ground, and in their place built Madinat al-Thawra, a huge low-income housing project just outside the capital. He also set up a program of low-interest loans to government workers, military officers, teachers, and other professionals to enable them to buy or build their own homes on small plots of land given to them by the government.

FOREIGN POLICY

Qassem's concern for the poor and his efforts to improve the quality of their lives won him much popular support, especially among the blue-collar working class. But he was much less successful in his foreign policy. He almost never traveled outside Iraq and had little personal knowledge of the outside world. As a result he made some serious mistakes in judgment, and these mistakes, along with failure to develop a strong base of support from the middle and upper classes in Iraqi society, eventually cost him his presidency and his life.

Qassem's most serious mistake in foreign policy involved Kuwait, Iraq's small southern neighbor. Kuwait ("little fort" in Arabic) had been for centuries a small mud-walled enclosure and harbor on the edge of the Arabian desert facing the Gulf. It was uninhabited except for occasional visits by nomadic tribes. However, one of these tribes settled there in the 1700s and began to develop it as a fishing port and boat-building center.

At that time the Ottoman empire included Kuwait as a part of the Iraqi province of Basra. However, the ruling chief (emir) of Kuwait paid an annual tribute to the governor of Basra and in turn was left in control of his territory. This arrangement continued until the late nineteenth century, when the emir stopped sending the tribute, saying it was an unnecessary drain on his finances. Fearing that the governor would send troops to occupy Kuwait, the emir signed a treaty with Great Britain to make his country a British protectorate.

In 1961, Britain granted independence to Kuwait, in line with British policy of withdrawing from its overseas possessions to reduce the cost of empire. The British also sponsored Kuwait for membership in the UN and the Arab League. The other Arab nations then welcomed Kuwait as a "brother nation," except for Iraq. Qassem said that Kuwait had been unfairly separated from his nation by imperialist powers, and he would send troops to restore rightful Iraqi rule over the lost province.

Britain promptly filed a complaint with the UN charging Iraq with a threat to world peace. However, the Arab League's members said that the Kuwait-Iraqi conflict was strictly an internal Arab matter. A peacekeeping force from various Arab countries was sent to Kuwait, and Qassem's declaration to invade the emirate proved to be an empty threat.

FALL OF THE "BLESSED LEADER"

Qassem's mismanagement of the dispute with Kuwait certainly cost him the support and friendship of other Arab governments. But his inability to reconcile the various groups and factions whose conflicts had always been an obstacle to national unity was the main cause of his downfall after a bare five years in power. He had already survived one assassination attempt in 1959, and a coup planned by disloyal army officers and supporters of 'Arif was thwarted only with the help of the well-organized Iraq Communist party (ICP). The support of the Communists turned away many formerly loyal army officers and Iraqi patriots, who felt that Qassem had "sold out" to a foreign ideology and power, namely the Soviet Union. But it was the outbreak of war in Kurdistan that put the final seal on Qassem's death warrant.

As noted earlier in this chapter, the provisional constitution issued after the 1958 revolution stated that Kurds and Arabs were partners in the new Iraqi republic.[23] The Kurds had supported the revolution, and their leader (*mullah*, a title of honor) Mustafa Barzani returned from years of exile in the Soviet Union to a public welcome in Baghdad.

But "partnership" had different meanings for Barzani and the Kurds than for Qassem. Barzani believed that it meant equality, with Kurds in charge of their own affairs, including the teaching of their language in schools, use of Kurdish along with Arabic on official documents, and protection of Kurdish culture, history, customs, and values as distinct from those of Arabs.

This was equal to a declaration of Kurdish independence from Iraq, and Qassem ordered the Iraqi army to invade Kurdistan. But Barzani's 5,000 Pesh Mergas (commandos or guerrillas) were more than a match for Iraqi army regulars. Using guerrilla tactics and operating from mountain hideouts, the Pesh Mergas ambushed army patrols, cut army supply lines, and isolated Iraqi garrisons in the northern cities. Iraqi planes bombed Kurdish villages as they would do in later campaigns, causing heavy casualties, but the bombings had the opposite effect of uniting the Kurds against the invaders, and more and more men joined the guerrillas.

By late 1962, Qassem had lost nearly all his political support. The army was demoralized by its failure to defeat the Pesh Mergas. Except for the Soviet Union, Iraq had almost no friends abroad. The Kuwait affair had made it more or less an outlaw nation, a role all too familiar in the 1990s. Most observers at the time thought that another revolution was in the making. But it was not clear how the overthrow of the popular "Blessed Leader" could be arranged, and what groups or organizations in Iraq's secretive, conflict-oriented society would unite to carry it out.

In view of these uncertainties the second Iraqi revolution was carried out with unexpected swiftness on February 8, 1963, the fourteenth day of the sacred Islamic month of Ramadan. Traditionally, Ramadan is a month devoted to prayer, fasting, and reconciliation with one's enemies. But Qassem's enemies were motivated more by their political concerns than by respect for Islamic belief and practice. They were a mixed lot—army officers frustrated by the failure of the Kurdish campaign, Arab nationalists determined to make Iraq the centerpiece of a greater Arab nation, student leaders, Communists, and members of the secret Ba'th party, an underground organization some of whose members had attempted to assassinate Qassem in 1959.

The revolution was carried out with military precision. Army units led by Qassem's rivals seized control of key bases, the Baghdad radio station, and other communications facilities with relative ease, since the bulk of the Iraqi army was tied down in Kurdistan. The Ministry of Defense building, where Qassem lived and worked (usually fourteen hours a day) was surrounded and its defenders overwhelmed after an all-day battle. Qassem was captured, strapped in a chair, and killed with a pistol shot to the head; there would be no trial for the head of state, merely instant revenge. Outside, in the streets and the poor neighborhoods of Baghdad, crowds who had supported and believed in him battled army tanks and infantry with sticks, stones, and pistols, before they were

Order was quickly restored after a military coup in 1963, but a rebel soldier keeps watch on the street to make sure.

mowed down and crushed. Hundreds died and many more were killed in later months as the revolutionaries set out to eliminate all who might oppose their rule.

Ironically, Qassem, in a speech shortly before his death, proposed a different course of action for his country, one that might have kept it from becoming the outlaw nation that it is today. He said: "Communists, Arab nationalists, democrats and others, I beg of you to remember that you are sons of the same country. Stop your futile quarrels and address yourselves above all to making Iraq a modern and prosperous country."[24]

The next chapter will examine the origins, structure, and history of the Arab Ba'th, the organization that has ruled Iraq since 1968, and its enigmatic absolute leader, Saddam Hussein.

CHAPTER SIX

LORD OF THE BA'TH

AT THE BEGINNING of the twenty-first century the Ba'th party has been in power in Iraq for more than three decades. In terms of the 8,000-year history of the land between the rivers, this period represents at best a blip on the screen of human life there. Yet it is a period of great importance to the Iraqi people. Of all the governments that have ruled Iraq since it was given its independence by the British and set on the road to becoming a modern nation, the Ba'th regime has been the only one able to create a specific Iraqi identity and sense of nationhood among the people.

However, the Ba'thist leaders did not acquire absolute power immediately. They had taken part in the overthrow and execution of Abdel Karim Qassem, but as one group along with others. The country's new leader, Colonel Abdel Salam 'Arif, was determined to keep power and to assure the control of the army over the government. To do so he built up a group of younger army officers who depended on him for their support. He also made a practice of appointing friends and relatives to key government

85

positions. He made no effort to develop a political system that would include all groups, and he paid little attention to the country's growing economic and social problems, the gap between rich and poor, for example. His one attempt to deal with these problems was to have his government take over all private banks, insurance companies, and large industrial plants such as steel mills; henceforth they would be managed by a national economic organization. This action, however, led to strikes and slowdowns in production as workers protested low wages and demanded the right to form unions.

'Arif was killed in a still-unexplained crash of his official helicopter in 1966 and was succeeded as president by his brother Abdel Rahman 'Arif, also an army officer. But the second 'Arif proved to be no better than the first in dealing with social and economic problems. Other groups joined the striking workers—doctors, nurses, teachers, university students, even tailors and garage mechanics. As a result Iraq's economic development came to a virtual stop.

The second 'Arif did manage to arrange a cease-fire with Barzani's Kurdish warriors, the Pesh Mergas, but only after they had defeated the Iraqi army in a major battle. The government then issued a formal declaration recognizing "Kurdish nationalism and Kurdish national rights within the bi-national character of the Iraqi state."[25] But the cease-fire did not hold up for long; army commanders were embarrassed by the poor showing of their troops and opposed to any long-term settlement agreement with Barzani; and the government's declaration of Iraq as a bi-national Arab-Kurdish state was little more than a meaningless gesture intended for world opinion.

Neither of the brothers took steps to establish a unified political system. Both of them had been helped to power by civilian groups. But once they had established their authority, they worked to weaken and even eliminate these groups. Thus Iraqi politics in the 1960s became "a game of alliances and counter-alliances, coups and countercoups, a frantic course to power" until such time as "there would arrive a strong party with a highly-structured organization, established before the rules of the game became out of date."[26]

MEET THE BA'TH

Two political organizations fit this description, the Iraqi Communist party (ICP) and the Ba'th. The ICP had been organized in the 1930s during the expansion of worldwide communism, and it had the benefit of an established ideology plus the guidance of Communist parties elsewhere, notably in the Soviet Union. However, it was supported in Iraq mainly by intellectuals rather than by practical politicians or military leaders. As Iraq progressed from mandate to kingdom and then to republic, the ICP played a small part in the process. Its best chance to seize power came after the 1958 revolution, when its leaders joined forces with Qassem to overthrow the monarchy. It fairly well controlled workers and "the street" with its urban mobs and demonstrators. However, Communist involvement in the 1959 assassination plot against Qassem turned the Blessed Leader against the party. His government worked with various groups to neutralize Communist control of labor and "the street." As historians Marion and Peter Sluglett noted, "The dilemma for the ICP was that of attempting to manage a political party in ways that would only work in a functioning democratic political system."[27] The party was broken up after the Ba'th takeover in 1968 and was officially banned (along with all other political parties) in 1978.

The Ba'th is another story. *Ba'th*, in Arabic, means "resurrection," and the party's original name was *al-Hizb al-Ba'th al-'Arabi* ("Party of the Arab Resurrection"). As its name implies, it is a group committed to uniting the various Arab peoples of the Middle East into a single Arab nation and throwing off the shackles of foreign rule.

The Arab Ba'th, as it is usually called, was founded in the 1940s in Syria. As was mentioned earlier, Syria became a self-declared independent Arab kingdom after World War I and was subsequently taken over as a mandate by the French. The Ba'th's founders were Michel 'Aflaq, a Greek Orthodox Christian, and Salah al-Din Bitar, a Sunni Muslim. They had grown up in the same neighborhood in Damascus, the Syrian capital, but owing to their different religious affiliations they did not know each other. They were educated in the separate schools of their religious faiths, and met when they were sent to France to study at the University of Paris. (It was a common practice during the mandate period for French officials to encourage well-to-do Syrian families to send their sons to Paris to be educated, so that they not only would learn European ways but also would be exposed to "superior" French customs and culture.)

'Aflaq and Bitar became acquainted in the course of their studies in Paris and even organized an Arab Students Union for the large numbers of young Arabs who had also come there from various countries to study. More important, their exposure to various thinkers and philosophers led them to develop a basic set of principles that would later become the guiding spirit of the Ba'th. This basic set of principles, in simplest terms, is Pan-Arabism—the unity, independence, and resurrection of the Arab peoples from the dustbin of history, the ashes of the past. 'Aflaq and Bitar brought these principles back to Syria and set to work putting them to practical use in forming a political organization that would unite the Arabs into a nation and bring European rule to an end.

Syria became independent of French rule in 1946 and began to chart its own course as a republic. However, the

Syrian population is similar to that of Iraq in being a mixture of ethnic, linguistic, religious, and other groups. The only organization capable of welding these groups into a unified and representative political system was the army. The army had been organized and trained by the French, but received little in the way of political guidance. Consequently, Syria's military leaders, like those of Iraq, were more interested in personal power than in representative government. In the years after independence, army officers carried out a series of coups against the civilian government. 'Aflaq and Bitar opposed these coups, and after Colonel Adib Shishakli overthrew his rivals and set up a military dictatorship, the two Ba'th leaders went into exile in neighboring Lebanon.

In Beirut, the Lebanese capital, they joined forces with Akram Hourani, the head of the small Syrian Arab Socialist party, who had also opted for exile. The party now acquired a new name, *al-Hizb al-Ba'th al-'Arabi al-Ishtiraki* ("Party of the Arab Socialist Resurrection") as socialism was added to its basic principle of Pan-Arabism.

In its early years the Ba'th attracted mostly professional people—writers, lawyers, teachers, and university professors, for example. But the merger with Hourani's party changed its membership to include army officers and village and tribal leaders. The majority of the Syrian

---

The charter or basic document of the Ba'th, as written by Michel 'Aflaq, defines it as follows: "The party of the Arab Ba'th is a socialist party. It believes that the economic wealth of the fatherland belongs to the Arab nation. Socialism arises from the depths of Arab nationalism. It makes up the ideal social order that will allow the Arab people to realize their possibilities, to enable their genius to flourish, and to ensure for the Arab nation constant progress."[28]

officers were Alawis, members of a minority group nominally considered as Shia Muslims but distrusted by both Shias and Sunnis because their rituals are secret and supposedly include observances of Christian holidays such as Christmas and Easter.

Unfortunately both for Syria and the Arab world in general, the Ba'thist principle and doctrine of Pan-Arabism proved more popular in theory than in practice. The Arab nations that became fully independent after World War II were led by military governments more interested in power for its own sake than in inter-Arab cooperation. And as was noted in Chapter Five, the establishment of the State of Israel in the "sacred Arab land" of Palestine and the defeat of Arab armies by the Israelis in several wars made the prospect of Arab unity more remote.

The Iraqi Ba'th inherited these negative prospects, which probably seemed more dismal at the time because of Iraq's own struggles to define itself as a modern nation and to organize a government of national unity. The party actually began as a branch of the Syrian Ba'th, and was formed in 1951 by Syrian teachers who had moved to Baghdad because of their opposition to Syria's military leaders. It had very few members in the early days. But in 1956, Michel 'Aflaq moved from Beirut to Baghdad. His presence in the Iraqi capital brought a tremendous increase in membership. By the time of the 1958 revolution the Ba'th could count on 1,200 full members (called "organized partisans"), 2,000 supporters, and 10,000 "sympathizers." Ba'thist partisans were actively involved in the opposition to Abdel Karim Qassem. But their first attempt to seize control of the government, in 1963, backfired as rival groups joined with President 'Arif and his fellow officers to remove all Ba'thist officials from power.

Having been driven from power, the Ba'th went underground for the next five years. But its leaders worked in secret to build a strong base of support, one that cut across social class and economic and political lines. They paid particular attention to the officer corps, encouraging officers who were sympathetic to their aims and principles to become secret members of the party. They laid the groundwork for a return to power with care, and their preparations were handsomely rewarded in July 1968, almost ten years to the day after the fall of the monarchy. The overthrow of 'Arif #2 was accomplished swiftly, efficiently, and almost without any bloodshed. One author noted that 'Arif was taken to the house of one of the Ba'thist leaders and given coffee and a bed for the night before leaving on a morning plane for exile![29]

This first completely Ba'th-controlled government of Iraq kept the facade of army involvement in politics as General Ahmed Hassan al-Bakr, a senior army officer and one of those who had been secretly a Ba'thist, was named president of the republic. But instead of the expected cabinet of ministers, which would have signaled Iraq's establishment of parliamentary government, supreme power was vested in a seven-member Revolution Command Council. (One of its members was a twenty-three-year-old street fighter whose only claim to fame was his participation in the 1959 assassination plot against Qassem. His name: Saddam Hussein.)

As was noted earlier in this chapter, the Iraqi Ba'th was formed as a branch of the Syrian Ba'th. By this time, however, the Syrian and Iraqi Ba'th parties had separated and were actually rivals, each claiming to be the rightful representative of the imaginary Arab nation. The Iraqi Ba'th had one advantage over the Syrian due to the presence of Michel 'Aflaq. After the 1968 coup, he was made secretary-general of the National Command, the unit of the Iraqi Ba'th responsible for inter-Arab relations, and he kept this position until his death in 1989. Ever since then the Iraqi Ba'th has claimed the right to speak for all the Arabs as their only true representative.

However, the Iraqi Ba'th's conversion into an Iraqi party has turned it away from Pan-Arabism toward Iraqi nationalism. Saddam Hussein noted in a speech in 1976 that "it should be our ambition to make all Iraqis Ba'thists in membership and beliefs." Although it is not yet a mass party, by the 1990s it had moved well beyond its original narrow base, with 30,000–50,000 full or "working" members and 1.5 million "sympathizers," about 8 percent of the total population.

How is the Iraqi Ba'th organized? Its secretive nature—left over from its underground years—and the Iraqi people's general distrust of foreigners (commented on by many visitors) make it very difficult to learn much about the inner workings of the party. During its years underground, it developed an organizational structure shaped like a pyramid. This structure seems to have been carried over, with the Revolution Command Council (RCC) at the topmost point. Below the RCC, in order of descent, are regional commands, subdivided into branches, sections, and divisions, with clusters of cells at the bottom. Each cell has three to seven members. In the past the members of one cell would not know those in another; all communications and directives were vertical, from top to bottom. But the elimination of all opposition and the Ba'th's status as the country's only legal political party have probably ended this isolation of cells from each other.

The motto of the Ba'th from its origins has been "Unity, Freedom, Socialism." The first step toward unity was taken in 1968 when the RCC issued a "temporary" constitution. This constitution defined Iraq as a popular democratic state whose bases are its Arab heritage and Islamic spirit. These terms were borrowed from European models and translated into Arabic (*dawla dimuqratiyya sha'biyya*). Thus they do not have the same meaning for Iraqis as they do for Americans. By the same token Iraq was made into a nation-state by the British rather than emerging naturally out of Iraqi Arab life and experience.

The RCC tried to resolve the problem of language terms in 1970 by approving a second "temporary" constitution. This one defined Iraq as a popular, democratic, sovereign republic, which was not much of an improvement on the first. In 1990 a third constitution was approved in principle, probably because Saddam Hussein (who held absolute power but by then had brought great hardship on his people due to his foreign-policy actions) wished to give the world the impression that he was moving toward a more open democratic system. The new constitution would allow political parties other than the Ba'th to form and would guarantee freedom of the press and human rights similar to those in the Western world. However, this "new" constitution has yet to be formally approved by the RCC and ratified by the National Assembly, a rubber-stamp parliamentary organization that the Iraqi leader had set up to demonstrate the move toward democracy.

THE BA'TH AND THE PEOPLE

In order to build up loyalty to the party and establish a permanent presence for the Ba'th in Iraq, party leaders have concentrated on certain groups, particularly young people and women. Saddam Hussein, in his 1976 speech, declared that "the young have a longer time to live; therefore they have a longer period to contribute to the work of the future as required by the revolutionary process of change."[30] Young Iraqis are exposed to Ba'thist beliefs and obligations from an early age. Boys and girls in primary schools are enrolled in the Pioneers, and between the ages of ten and fifteen they move on to the Vanguard (formed in 1973). Those over the age of sixteen are eligible for membership in the party but only after a training period, which can last up to seven years in various stages. These stages are highly competitive. Those who make it to the very top of the pyramid (the RCC) do so not only by per-

A young girl Vanguard member recites patriotic verse.

formance but also through total loyalty to the party and active participation in all of its programs.

As noted above, indoctrination for the young starts early and continues through high school. Boys and girls alike wear blue camouflage-style uniforms to school, begin the school day with the pledge of allegiance "to the Ba'th and the Iraqi nation," and are required to engage in out-of-school supervised competitive sports, notably soccer. At the Vanguard level they meet weekly in small groups (cells) and are instructed in Ba'thist ideology by regular party members. Their school textbooks emphasize the glorious Iraqi past, all the way back to Mesopotamia and its brilliant future under the leadership of the Ba'th. Iraq's wars have reinforced its image as a frontier state isolated from the outside world yet unique in its Ba'thist pride. Thus, a foreign journalist noted during a visit to an elementary school that when the teacher asked the children to state their goals in life, one of them answered "to be a soldier and grow up to be a soldier of our country."[31]

Women are the other social group most affected by the Ba'thist transformation of Iraq into a unified nation. A party report in 1974 stated: "The liberation of the Arab woman from her antiquated economic, social, and legal bonds is one of our main aims; the Party has a leading role to play in the liberation of women since it [is important] in the process of social and cultural change."[32] After it came to power in 1968 the Ba'th organized the General Federation of Iraqi Women (GFIW) to "mobilize Iraqi women in the struggle of the nation against reaction and backwardness," and subsequently issued a Code of Personal Status to give women rights similar to those in Western countries in such areas of life as marriage, divorce, and child custody. Other laws issued by the RCC established good working conditions for women, paid maternity leave and childcare for employed mothers, and equality with men in the workplace in pay and other benefits.

These laws and the leadership of the GFIW have led to active participation by women in both party and national life. By 1980 women made up 46 percent of all teachers, 46 percent of dentists, and 70 percent of pharmacists, for example. Women are active in the party at all levels except that of the RCC, which remains an exclusive "men's club." And women have far more freedom in Iraq than in other, more rigidly Islamic states such as Saudi Arabia. They drive their own cars, work outside the home, go unveiled in public, vote, and are members of the

National Assembly. And as was the case in the United States during World War II, Iraqi women in the 1980s and 1990s have had to participate in large numbers in industries and businesses due to the large number of male casualties during the 1980–1988 war between Iran and Iraq.

LORD OF THE BA'TH

Saddam who? The rhetorical question at the beginning of this book that underscored how little Americans knew of Iraq in the late 1970s is irrelevant today. A check on the Internet lists 18,000 references to Saddam Hussein, and hardly a day passes without media attention to his joustings with the UN and the United States in his efforts to remove the economic straitjacket placed on Iraq as an outlaw nation.

Yet not so long ago Saddam Hussein was not only unknown outside Iraq but almost unknown to his own countrymen. Those who knew or dealt with him saw him as a minor figure in a secret opposition party, which was outside the mainstream of power.

What do we know about Saddam Hussein outside the glare of media publicity, about his background and the people and experiences that shaped his life? The details are sparse and often conflicting. The Iraqi leader has played many roles in public life and has invented many stories about himself, even including family descent from the caliph Ali, the Prophet Muhammad's son-in-law and model for Shia Islam. But what we know of Saddam Hussein's life suggests a pattern of the rise from obscurity to supreme power, the "rags to riches" story often associated with success in America.

The future Lord of the Ba'th was born in 1937 in a mud hut with a roof of reeds in a village near the large town of

Tikrit, about 100 miles (160 kilometers) south of Baghdad on the Tigris River. He was given the name Saddam, meaning "he who confronts and is bold," at birth. His father had died shortly before he was born, and his mother married her late husband's brother in accordance with Islamic and tribal custom. In his early years young Saddam tended sheep, and there is some evidence that his stepfather also abused him. Whatever the truth, at the age of ten the young shepherd ran away to live in Tikrit with an uncle.

Saddam's uncle, Tulfah, had served in the British-trained Iraqi army and had taken part in the 1941 Rashid Ali revolt against British rule. When the revolt failed he was dismissed from the army and given a five-year jail sentence. The experience embittered the ex-officer, and he passed along his anger and hatred of the British in particular and foreigners in general to his nephew. Tulfah also filled the young man's mind with stories of the greatness of the Arabs in the days of the caliphs of Baghdad. Some day you will lead our people back to greatness, he told his nephew in what might be considered a prophecy.

Young Saddam attended school in Tikrit, but he was apparently a poor student and absent a good deal of the time. In 1955, when he was eighteen, his uncle moved with his family to Baghdad. As noted in Chapter Four, the Iraqi capital at that time was filled with plots and rumors of plots against the British-sponsored monarchy and particularly against the much-disliked regent, who was still ruling the country because of Faisal II's young age. Many young Iraqis at that time took their cue from Egypt, where army officers led by Colonel Gamal Abdel Nasser had overthrown the monarchy and established a republic. The young Iraqis began demonstrating in the streets of Baghdad to demand the ouster of the British and the overthrow of the monarchy in favor of an Iraqi republic similar to Egypt's.

Saddam Hussein had been encouraged by his uncle to apply for admission to the Baghdad Military Academy and work to become an officer in the army. But he was turned down because of poor grades and failure to finish high school. At loose ends, he began to take part in the student demonstrations, swaggering around Baghdad with a pistol tucked inside his shirt. At the age of twenty he joined the Ba'th party and began the long, slow climb in its ranks.

The party's new recruit did not take part in the 1958 revolution. But in 1959 he was one of a group of young Ba'thist guerrillas assigned to assassinate Abdel Karim Qassem. The attempt failed. Accounts differ concerning his part in it, but all agree that he was wounded in the leg, escaped across the border to Syria, and eventually made his way to Cairo, Egypt. He finished high school in Cairo and entered law school there, but seems to have spent most of his time sitting in a local restaurant, drinking tea and picking fights with other patrons. (Years later the restaurant owner commented that he could not believe that such a bully and braggart, who was always picking fights, could become president of Iraq!)

The bully had been given a fifteen-year jail term for his part in the assassination attempt, but when Qassem was killed in 1963, Saddam hurried home to Iraq. He was given a minor job in the party's organization, something like chief of the bureau of peasants. When the Ba'th was driven from the government by President 'Arif, Saddam was arrested and spent two years behind bars, escaping in 1966. From then on he worked hard to rebuild his party, on the basis of three principles: (1) never share power with another group; (2) keep the army out of politics; and (3) avoid factions and rivalries that break up the leadership. He learned these lessons well, and they are the main reason for his tenure as the supreme leader of his country.

After the Ba'th came to power in 1968, Saddam Hussein worked slowly and carefully to build a power base for himself. He organized the security and intelligence services—the "long arm" of the party that would eventually reach into almost every home in Iraq with its network of spies, agents, and informers. He also formed a popular militia similar to the U.S. National Guard but in Iraq intended to neutralize the influence of the army in politics.

Ironically, it was President al-Bakr, an army officer as well as a Ba'thist, who arranged for the elimination of the officer corps from the government. He seems to have adopted Saddam Hussein as his protégé, and their relationship became more of a father and son than that of a leader and his second in command. But as time passed in the 1970s, Saddam took over more of the responsibilities of government from the ailing al-Bakr. He arranged the nationalization of the Iraq Petroleum Company in 1972, and in the same year signed a treaty of cooperation with the Soviet Union to modernize the Iraqi armed forces with huge purchases of Russian tanks, planes, and other weapons of war, along with Russian advisers to retrain the army in Soviet techniques.

By 1979, Saddam Hussein was ready to become the Lord of the Ba'th. President al-Bakr was seriously ill, suffering from diabetes and heart problems. On July 16 he announced his resignation. His deputy, the chairman of the RCC and thus the second most important person in the country and the Ba'th party, would succeed him as president of the republic. The onetime *shaqawah* ("bully" in the dialect of Tikrit) was now not only the titular but also the real ruler of Iraq.

BROTHERS AND ENEMIES

"THE REVOLUTION CHOOSES ITS ENEMIES." —Saddam Hussein

During the first two decades of his rule, Saddam Hussein survived two major wars, an unknown number of plots against him by rivals at home, sanctions imposed by the UN that have crippled Iraq's economy and brought great suffering to its people, and even limits to its sovereign right to control its own territory. He is distrusted by many world leaders, including some of his fellow Arab heads of state, and considered by U.S. foreign-policy experts as the principal threat to world peace. Yet he continues to survive, bobbing and weaving like a lightweight boxer faced with a heavier opponent and striking blows where they are least expected. How can this situation be explained? What is there about the nation of Iraq and its leader that enables them to stand up against the weight of the world?

To consider these questions, and in the light of Iraq's modern history as an artificial nation formed out of conflicting groups, the relationship forged between ruler and people must be examined. An Iraqi poet described this relationship in a poem written for children to sing in school:

> "We are Iraq and its name is Saddam;
> We are a people and its name is Saddam;
> We are love and its name is Saddam;
> We are the Ba'th and its name is Saddam."[33]

Not long after the temporary end of the Gulf War (discussed in Chapter Eight) a Baghdad newspaper commented in an editorial: "We have Saddam and they have their democracy. Let them enjoy this democracy; we are content to have an Arab leader, a Muslim seeker of peace, Saddam Hussein, may God preserve him." As these examples suggest, Iraq's long and difficult struggle to become a nation with a specific national identity, a real sense of nationhood, has ended in one-man rule. But it is a rule that for better or worse unites leader and people. Admittedly, this state (officially a republic) falls far short of meeting the American definition of a democracy, let alone a republic. But in terms of building a nation out of extremely unpromising materials, the difference between Saddam Hussein and his predecessors is that he has made the process work.

THE CARROT AND THE STICK

How did Saddam manage to do so? One explanation is his use of the analogy of the carrot and the stick, originally applied by the peasant to his donkey to make it move. Saddam's "carrot" was to surround himself with loyal supporters, many of them relatives or natives of Tikrit, his adopted hometown. He rewarded them with special privileges and perks—fine cars, elegant homes, and large salaries, for example. At the same time he made sure they knew the source of these perks and that none of them would use their status to build up a rival power base to threaten his rule. "If I die you will all die with me," he once warned the other members of the RCC. He was especially distrustful of military commanders; an underlying reason behind his aggressive foreign-policy actions was to keep the army occupied and its leaders out of politics. Yet he was careful to avoid allowing any of them to become national heroes. The general who commanded the successful reconquest of the Fao Peninsula during the war with Iran (discussed later in this chapter) was dismissed from the army and sent home because he had acted on his own initiative and did not give Saddam the credit for the action.

The "stick" was used more often than the carrot. Saddam's method of control combined brutality with terror to a much greater degree than any of his predecessors. Violence was natural to him not only because he suffered childhood abuse but also because he spent his adult life as a member of the Ba'th mostly on the run. As was noted earlier, the Ba'thists saw themselves as surrounded by the enemies of the Arab nation, in a worldwide conspiracy to destroy it. They carried this view with them when they came out of the shadows to win power.

The use of violence under Saddam has turned Iraq into a huge prison, although in our less-than-perfect world this imprisonment provides Iraqis with stability in return for repression of all democratic freedoms. Execution of opponents at home and abroad is official Ba'th policy: "The long arm of the revolution will reach out to its enemies wherever they are found," Saddam Hussein has said, and in the 1970s and early 1980s a number of exiled leaders and "enemies of the state" (such as Israeli diplomats) were killed or targeted for death by Ba'thist agents.

The "climate of fear" that has pervaded the country as a result of this system of repression has made verification difficult. But shortly after he became president, Saddam Hussein announced that a plot to overthrow him by certain members of the RCC had been discovered. He held a party meeting at which one of the accused made a public "confession" implicating others. As their names were read they were seized by guards, taken from the meeting room, and shot, while Saddam sat impassively in the head chair smoking an expensive cigar. Some twenty-two party leaders were eliminated in this manner, and the proceedings videotaped and sent to other Arab heads of state to "help them understand the need for the Ba'th to destroy enemies within its ranks."[34]

Saddam's use of the carrot-and-stick technique extends even to his own relatives. In 1995 two of his sons-in-law, his daughters, and a number of army officers fled to neighboring Jordan. One of them had been defense minister and the mastermind of Iraq's nuclear and chemical/biological weapons program. He said he had lost faith in the Lord of the Ba'th and would organize a campaign to overthrow him. However, the group was considered suspect by the Jordanian government, and in 1996 most of its members returned to Iraq, saying they had changed their minds and were loyal to Iraq. Saddam said they would be pardoned as "repentant sinners." But after their return the daughters divorced their husbands, who then were shot as "enemies of the state."

THE MYTHMAKER

Saddam Hussein has also cultivated an image of himself as the symbol of the Iraqi nation. To do so he plays many roles. He is the typical peasant in the *aba* (traditional long robe of rural Iraqis) threshing wheat on a cooperative farm; the commander in chief reviewing troops in full uniform with medals, beret, and sunglasses; a worker carrying

Here, Saddam Hussein wears traditional attire.

cement or bricks in the rebuilding of ancient Babylon. Prior to the Gulf War and the resulting years of sanctions, he might be found at weddings or circumcision ceremonies with ordinary people, drinking coffee in the tents of nomadic Turkoman tribesmen, or visiting an outdoor market to inspect the quality of its fruits and vegetables. When receiving foreign officials he wore Western tailored suits and ties, and although the Ba'th downplays Islam as a religious force he arranged to be photographed during the annual pilgrimage to Mecca, wearing the white seamless robe required of pilgrims to the sacred city. With the help of the U.S. media, Saddam's name has become a household word in America, but it is his face that is most familiar in Iraq, in thousands of posters 20 feet (6 meters) high at airport entrances, in banks and public buildings, on bus-stop waiting stands, on hillsides, and even on billboards in vacant lots. Almost the only joke that circulates in Iraq is the one that goes: "What is the population? Twenty-one million Iraqis and twenty-one million portraits of Saddam."[35]

Saddam uses mythmaking also to link himself with the past, to remind his people of their historic glories, real

Larger-than-life posters of Saddam Hussein can be seen nearly everywhere. This mural depicts Saddam in military dress as he overlooks Iraq's military, industrial, and energy strengths.

or imagined. He is the modern Hammurabi, the new Nebuchadnezzar, builder of Babylon and conqueror of the ancient Jews. In 1990 investigators of family trees "discovered" that he was descended from the caliph Ali, the Prophet Muhammad's son-in-law, and he has often compared himself with Saladin, the Islamic warrior (actually a Kurd but also from Tikrit) who drove the Christian Crusaders from Palestine.

THE ECONOMIC BOOM

The other important contribution of the Ba'thist regime to the well-being of the Iraqi people prior to Saddam's disastrous foreign-policy initiatives was in economic development. The oil industry was nationalized, and both production and exports increased enormously. By 1979 oil production was 3.4 million barrels per day, and revenues had reached $26 billion. This vast new wealth made possible many large-scale development projects. Paved highways now crisscrossed the land between the rivers, and blocks of apartment buildings ringed Baghdad and other cities to house rural peasants seeking to work in factories and escape the poverty and toil of farm life. Baghdad also had skyscraper office buildings, elegant modern hotels, a world-class conference center, and forty-five shopping malls to go along with its traditional outdoor market and the gleaming domes and minaret towers of its Great Mosque.

Many of these projects were associated directly with Saddam as the great Benefactor of his country. In addition to his billboard portraits, his name was stamped on bridges and other public-works projects, even on every hundredth brick used in the rebuilding of Babylon. He was especially generous to his adopted hometown: Tikrit was transformed from a dusty town to a metropolis with paved streets, a hospital and university, and a museum where the faithful could come and peer at memorabilia of the childhood and youth of the Supreme Leader.

As the result of this boom, Iraq by 1980 was well on its way to self-sufficiency—the ability of a modern nation to meet all its needs without having to import goods, materials, and the services of foreign experts required for continued economic development.

The economic boom also brought about a large middle class of educated businessmen and professionals—doctors, lawyers, teachers, and government workers. Universities were built in other cities to relieve enrollment at the long-established University of Baghdad, along with teacher-training colleges and technical institutes throughout the country. By 1980 about 80 percent of Iraq's people could read and write.

FOREIGN RELATIONS

Progress and prosperity, however, became distant memories after 1980 when Saddam Hussein set out to make Iraq the dominant power in the region and the larger Arab world beyond its borders. He did so from what might be called a blinkered vision of the world outside Iraq, along with an obsessive drive to restore the Arab peoples to their long-lost central position in the time of the caliphs of Baghdad. And this faulty understanding of world politics, along with a misreading of history, has had serious consequences for his country and people.

The first move came in September 1980. Six Iraqi divisions swept across the border with neighboring Iran in a surprise attack, seizing the Iranian (east) bank of the Shatt al-Arab and capturing Iran's westernmost province of Khuzestan. The Iraqi commander in chief told his men that they were taking part in "Saddam's Qadisiya," the modern version of the great Arab victory over the Persians thirteen centuries earlier. He said the war would be over in a month, when the Iranians would surrender, and they would come and celebrate with their families.

Behind the invasion lay a long history of Iraqi-Iranian conflict. As was noted in Chapter Three, Iran has been officially a Shia Islamic state since the sixteenth century, while Ottoman Turkish leaders worked with the Sunni Arabs in Iraq to control its large Shia population. Also, despite the Arab victory at Qadisiya and conversion of the Iranians to Islam, the latter have always regarded Arabs as newcomers to civilization, having nothing to compare with Iran's 2,500 years of high culture.

In the twentieth century political issues were added to Iraqi-Iranian social rivalry. The British, as sponsors of the newly independent kingdom, asked the League of Nations to include the Shatt al-Arab, from bank to bank, in Iraq's territory, on the grounds that otherwise the country would be landlocked. Iran, in contrast, had a long coastline and numerous ports on the Gulf. The League agreed, and in 1937 approved Iraq's ownership of the entire waterway.

In 1969, however, the shah (ruler) of Iran denounced the award. He said that Iran's ships should have the right to use the Shatt from the east (Iranian) bank to mid-channel, without interference or having to pay tolls or taxes to Iraq. By this time both countries had become major oil producers, and free use of the waterway was essential to their oil exports. Due to its much larger population and its more powerful army, equipped with the latest in U.S. weapons, Iran was able to do so. In 1971, Iranian commandos occupied three small islands controlling the Strait of Hormuz (which connects the Shatt al-Arab with the Gulf and the Indian Ocean) as further proof of Iran's dominance over its neighbor.

The two countries also were at odds over Iraq's Kurdish population. In the early 1970s the shah began supplying Barzani's Pesh Mergas with modern weapons. His purpose was to keep Iraq weak and preoccupied with internal problems, tying its forces down in a conflict they could not win, against a determined enemy in difficult mountain terrain.

The shah's plan worked well, but in 1975 he changed his mind. Iran's long-range interests were now more important than support for an Iraqi minority people. He signed an agreement with the Ba'th, called the Algiers Agreement because it was worked out with the help of Algerian negotiators in Algiers, capital of Algeria. The shah agreed to stop sending weapons to the Iraqi Kurds, and in return Iraq accepted the principle of the midchannel line of the Shatt al-Arab as the boundary between the two countries. Kurdish resistance collapsed, and Iranian oil tankers now moved freely down the Iranian side of the waterway.

Saddam Hussein had signed the Algiers Agreement, but he felt he had done so out of Iraqi weakness and had given away sacred Arab territory. (He even had a booklet printed for schoolchildren. The text read: "Have you ever heard of a thief trying to steal a river? The Persians are trying to do just that, claiming that the Shatt al-Arab is half theirs.") He brooded over ways to get even with Iraq's ancient enemies.

Then, unexpectedly, in 1979 fate gave him a golden opportunity. The all-powerful shah was overthrown by a popular revolution, and Iran was now an Islamic republic, the first of its kind in the modern world. Young Iranians had occupied the American embassy in Teheran, Iran's capital, and were holding Americans there as hostages. As a result Iran had become an outlaw nation for its violation of international law. And the once-powerful Iranian army was in a shambles. It had been armed by the shah and was fiercely loyal to him, and his overthrow and departure for exile seriously affected army morale.

Saddam Hussein also had a personal bone to pick with the Iranians. The leader of the popular revolution was a frail, bearded eighty-year-old religious scholar named Ruhollah Musavi Khomeini, the highest-ranking member of the body of Shia religious leaders who had been in charge of the revolution. As with Saddam Hussein in the 1990s, this scholar's name would become known worldwide in the 1980s, especially by his title, *Ayatollah* ("Sign of God").

Khomeini had been exiled by the shah in 1963 because of his outspoken opposition to and criticism of the shah's modernization program for Iran. Saddam Hussein gave him refuge and allowed him to live in the Shia holy city of Najaf, where he gave lectures and continued to denounce the shah in cassettes and booklets smuggled into Iran. But after the Algiers Agreement, Khomeini was no longer welcome in Iraq. In 1978, Saddam shipped him off to Paris, France, from where he directed the revolution. In 1979 he returned to Iran on the heels of the departing shah to become the supreme leader of the new Islamic republic.

BROTHER ENEMIES

The upheaval in Iran seemed the perfect time for Saddam Hussein to avenge himself on Khomeini for the latter's abuse of Iraqi hospitality. Also the Islamic republic under Khomeini was committed to an active policy of exporting its "Islamic revolution" to other Muslim countries. Saddam feared that if given half a chance, the large Shia population in Iraq would rise against his government and establish a similar government, perhaps even restore the age-old Iranian control. He told his troops that they were the first line of Arab defense against the "yellow wind" of Iranian invasion and would be invading Iran to help its population overthrow the "traitor and unbeliever" Khomeini.

In addition to Iran's presumed military weakness, Saddam Hussein assumed that the predominantly Arab population of Khuzestan would welcome the invasion and join Iraqi troops on the march to Teheran. But this did not happen; Khuzestan's Arab population preferred the relatively light control of the distant Iranian government to the harsh hand of the Ba'th. The Iranian army performed better than expected, especially as its leaders proclaimed a *jihad* (holy war) against Saddam as a traitor to Islam and an unbeliever. The *jihad* brought thousands of volunteers, the great majority of them teenagers. Inspired by religious fervor, they attacked Iraqi lines in vast human waves, lightly armed and wearing red headbands stamped "Warriors of God." The Iraqi guns mowed them down, wave after wave, but still they came, gradually wearing down the tired Iraqi defenders.

The expected one-month war went on for years, with advances and retreats from fixed positions and occasional surprise raids. In 1982, Saddam Hussein declared a cease-fire and asked for peace negotiations. But Khomeini would have none of it. He said his goal was the removal of the "traitor to Islam." It would take six more years and useless expenditure of many more lives before outside powers could mediate an end to the war.

By 1987 the battle between Islamic brothers had become a matter of international concern. Iraq's use of chemical weapons against the Iranians violated international law, and its missile attacks on Iranian cities had brought the war home to the civilian population. Also air battles over the Gulf threatened the oil supply to Western Europe and the United States, and experts feared that chemical and biological weapons, "the atomic bombs of the poor," might easily fall into the hands of terrorists. In July the UN Security Council approved Resolution 598.

It called for a cease-fire, withdrawal of all forces behind their borders, and immediate negotiations for a complete peace settlement. Saddam Hussein agreed to the terms, but Khomeini took a full year to do so. He had sworn to fight to the last drop of his blood, but he finally said, "I drink this cup of bitter poison and submit to the will of God as a true Muslim." A year later he was dead.

The eight-year war left both economies in ruins; the cost to Iraq was about $450 billion. The death toll totaled nearly a million, plus 1–2 million wounded. In the early years the Iraqi government had been able to cushion the impact on the population through borrowing from currency reserves and the financial support of Arab oil-producing states. But as the battle went on and on, Iraq's development came to a halt. Saddam had promised the families of the *shahids* (martyrs) killed in battle that they would receive $30,000 each, but funds were not even available for those who had presumably died for their country.

KILLING THE KURDS

"Level the mountains in a day,
and the Kurds would be no more."
Kurdish proverb

As the war with Iran dragged to its close, Saddam Hussein cast his cold eye on Iraqi Kurdistan. The region had remained relatively quiet after the collapse of the resistance; the Pesh Mergas had either taken refuge in Turkey or Iran or were holed up in remote mountain hideouts. But as Iraqi garrisons were withdrawn to fight on the Iranian front, the Pesh Mergas gradually filtered back to regain partial control of their homeland. By the mid-1980s, Iraqi troops held the cities but only during the day; the Pesh Mergas ruled at night.

Kurdish forces also began taking part regularly in Iranian attacks on Iraqi towns near the border. After one such raid had destroyed one of Saddam's palaces, the Lord of the Ba'th decided on drastic measures. He would figuratively "level the mountains" to destroy the Kurds as a people. His plan had echoes of the "Final Solution" devised by Adolf Hitler and other German Nazi leaders to eliminate the Jewish population of occupied Europe during World War II. Saddam's plan was carried out with the same ruthless efficiency plus certain refinements.

According to historian Raul Hilberg, three steps are necessary for the elimination of a people: definition, concentration or seizure, and annihilation or extermination. Saddam's plan followed these three steps. They were carried out in successive stages in 1987–1988, and with the Iraqi leader's preference for suitable historical Islamic names, the operation against the Kurds was code-named *Anfal*, meaning "spoils of war" in Arabic.[36] The use of the Koranic term was intended to justify the slaughter of the Kurds because of their hostility to the Iraqi Islamic state. The campaign was directed by Saddam's cousin, Minister of Defense Ali Hassan al-Majid, known to this day as Ali Anfal, or "Chemical Ali," to the Kurds because of his authorization of the use of chemical weapons against them.

Chemical Ali issued standing orders for the stages of Anfal. All male Kurds were automatically identified as Pesh Mergas, subject to arrest and execution without trial. Their families were to be relocated in camps far from Kurdistan, and their villages burned and bulldozed over to leave no trace. No compensation would be provided for the displaced Kurdish families; they would be hauled in trucks to camps in the desert and left there to starve or die.

As a result of the campaign about 50,000 Kurds were killed, thousands of villages destroyed, and thousands of women, children, and the elderly relocated under appalling conditions far from their native mountains. About 60,000 Kurds escaped to Turkey, where they were held in relocation camps while the Turkish government struggled to care for them with its own limited resources. For all practical purposes the ancient rural economy of the Kurds in their mountains had been ruined by Anfal.

Despite the disregard of Anfal for human rights and the dignity of human beings, the Iraqi government did not hide its campaign from the world. Its actions were justified as necessary to overcome internal opposition—that is, the refusal of the Kurds to accept its authority over northern Iraq. However, documents captured after the 1991 Gulf War and the renewed uprising in Kurdistan (see Chapter Eight) describe a pattern of mass murders, gross violations of human rights, and use of chemical weapons against a civilian population far in excess of the amount of force actually needed. For these reasons Anfal was an action of genocide, the elimination of a particular group or people. The term was first used in the trial of Nazi leaders in Nuremberg, Germany, after World War II. The UN defined it in a 1951 convention as a crime under international law—"actions committed with intent to destroy in whole or in part a national, ethnic, racial or religious group as such." One of Saddam Hussein's "refinements" was the use of chemical weapons on Kurdish towns and cities; altogether some seventy such attacks were reported, the best known being the killing of 5,000 Kurds in the border town of Halabja in March 1988 by bombs with a deadly mixture of mustard and cyanide gases. Inasmuch as Iraq had signed the Convention Against Genocide as well as the earlier (1925) Geneva Protocol outlawing the use of chemical weapons, Iraq's president and his regime stand accused of crimes against international law and of violating the most basic human rights of its own people.

CHAPTER EIGHT

AT WAR WITH THE WORLD

**"WHAT IS AT STAKE** is more than one small country; it is a new world order, where diverse nations are drawn together in common cause, to achieve the universal aspirations of mankind: peace and security, freedom and the rule of law."

President George Bush,
State of the Union Address,
1991

Almost ten years to the day after he had sent his army into Iran, Saddam Hussein overturned the "new world order" with another bold stroke. This time the move was directed at a neighboring "brother Arab" state, the emirate of Kuwait. On August 2, 1990, battle-seasoned Iraqi troops swept across the desert border between the two countries, crushing the small Kuwaiti army under its superior weaponry.

Iraq's invasion of Kuwait is often described as a textbook example of aggression, and with respect to Bush's "new world order" it is an appropriate description. In international relations, the fall of the Berlin Wall dividing

117

West from East Germany, and the breakup of the Soviet Union into separate nations, left the United States as the world's only superpower. American foreign-policy makers had hoped that the Soviet breakup would enable the nations of the world to unite under U.S. leadership and work together toward the goals outlined in Bush's State of the Union address. But as might have been predicted, instead of unity the world was beset with new or revived conflicts, not only between nations but also within national borders. The Iraqi attack on Kuwait was described as an internal affair between "brother Arabs," but like a stone skipped across a pond, it cast ever-widening circles until most of the world was involved.

Why did Saddam invade Kuwait? On the surface his timing could not have been worse. Iraq had just ended an eight-year war that had drained its resources and caused a huge number of casualties. With the Soviet Union no longer in existence, Iraq had lost its major arms supplier and international patron. Relations with the United States were vastly improved. The American embassy in Baghdad had reopened after a seventeen-year break, and as a result of the "tilt" toward Iraq in its war with Iran the United States began supplying sophisticated military equipment, such as guides for missiles, to the Iraqi army. Also, the State Department had removed Iraq from its list of countries sponsoring international terrorism, enabling it to purchase surplus American wheat and other commodities for its growing population.

But Iraq's leader has been a gambler and risk-taker all his life. Bold, unexpected moves are his trademark; they were brought out to perfection in the attack on Kuwait. One other consistent element in his character is his commitment to and belief in the concept of the great Arab nation. In his mind this nation is not fragmented into individual countries but represents a single unit, struggling to find its place in the modern world yet mindful of its brilliant ancient past. As he has said in speeches, "the glory of the Arabs stems from the glory of Iraq. When Iraq became mighty and flourished, so did the Arab nation. When Iraq declined and came under foreign occupation, so did the Arab nation." The reattachment of Kuwait to Iraq, in his view, represented an important step toward rebuilding the Arab nation under Iraqi leadership.

THE OCCUPATION OF KUWAIT

The Lebanese scholar Fouad Ajami has commented on the difference between the Arabs of the north (Arab al-Shimal) and the Arabs of the Gulf (Arab al-Khalij; that is, south) as a factor hampering Arab unity. Those in the north live in a state of perpetual feud, and those of the Gulf in an orderly society governed by merchants and patriarchal rulers, he says.[37] Saddam's seizure of Kuwait overturned this orderly society, bringing chaos and violence into Gulf Arab life and seriously damaging the cause of Arab unity.

As noted in Chapter Five, earlier Iraqi governments had made claims to Kuwait. But Saddam was the first to back up the claim with force. It was no contest; the Iraqi army overran the emirate in seven hours, possibly a record for an act of aggression by one country against another. Kuwait's rulers and high officials managed to escape ahead of the advancing Iraqis and formed a government-in-exile, while a previously unknown "Provisional Government of Free Kuwait" appeared mysteriously and demanded to be annexed by Iraq, as its nineteenth province. Saddam announced: "This part and branch of the dear Arab homeland is now returned to the whole and root, Iraq, in comprehensive, eternal and inseparable unity."[38]

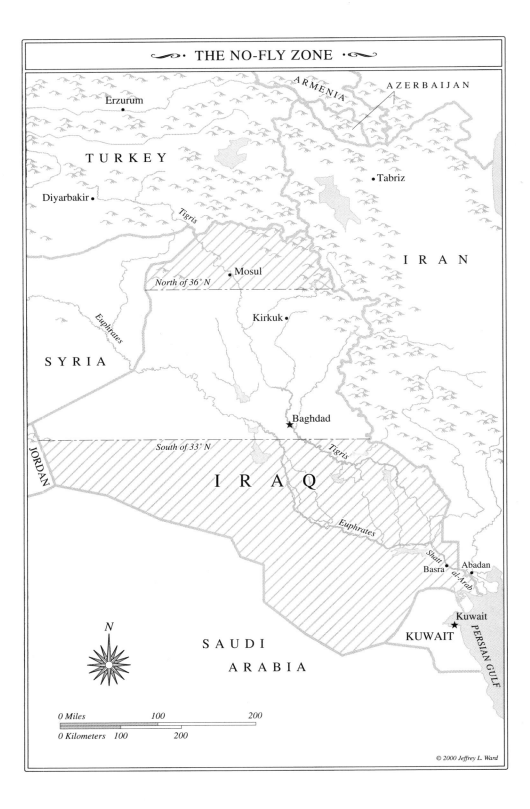

THE NO-FLY ZONE

Erzurum

ARMENIA

AZERBAIJAN

TURKEY

Tabriz

Diyarbakir

Tigris

IRAN

North of 36° N

Mosul

SYRIA

Euphrates

Kirkuk

Baghdad

JORDAN

South of 33° N

Tigris

IRAQ

Euphrates

Shatt al-Arab

Basra

Abadan

N

Kuwait

SAUDI

KUWAIT

PERSIAN GULF

ARABIA

0 Miles   100   200

0 Kilometers   100   200

© 2000 Jeffrey L. Ward

On the ground in occupied Kuwait the picture was much grimmer, as Iraqi soldiers swarmed over the emirate like killer bees. Many of them were simple country boys unused to the wealth and glittering luxury of the oil-rich Kuwaiti state. They rampaged for days, looting, burning, and killing not only Kuwaitis suspected of resistance but also foreign workers. Anything that could be moved was piled into army trucks, weapons carriers, even tanks, and carted back to Baghdad to be sold or given to their families. The loot included Mercedes cars, traffic lights, fully equipped research laboratories, a complete telephone system, even the emir's prize stable of race horses. A Kuwaiti poet in exile mourned for her lost homeland:

"Who killed Kuwait?
The killer did not descend from the sky
Or emerge from a world of dreams.
He who killed Kuwait is our own flesh and blood;
He is the embodiment of all our ways.
We made him to our own measurements." [39]

THE WORLD REACTS

Word of the Iraqi invasion reached Washington, D.C., early on a humid night in August. Most of President Bush's top foreign-policy advisers had gone home, and few expected that Saddam's threat to annex an Arab neighbor and endanger the new and mutually beneficial ties with the United States was anything more than a bluff. Also, the Bush administration had given Saddam the impression that his dealings with Kuwait were of no concern to them; that they were a dispute between Arabs and not a threat to world peace. In an earlier meeting with Saddam, the U.S. ambassador, April Glaspie, had seemingly confirmed that impression. "We have no opinion on inter-Arab disputes," she was quoted as saying, "such as your border dispute with Kuwait. My instructions are to seek better relations with Iraq, and to assure you that there are no American conspiracies against your country."[40]

Other Arab leaders were also surprised by the invasion, especially as Saddam had assured them that he was a man of peace. The Arab country most alarmed was Saudi Arabia. That oil-rich country had bankrolled Iraq during its war with Iran, and Saudi leaders could not believe that Saddam would damage relations with his main benefactor. Now with a large Iraqi army poised on their border with Kuwait, the Saudis feared that their turn would be next.

This possibility spurred the United States into action. Saudi oil exports were essential to the motor-driven U.S. economy as well as those of the nations of Europe. Successive U.S. presidents going back to Franklin D. Roosevelt had cultivated close relations with the desert kingdom in order to protect the supply of oil, and in return Saudi Arabia had received modern weapons in huge amounts from American manufacturers. However, the small Saudi army was incapable of resisting an Iraqi attack and would presumably lose all these modern weapons if the Iraqis came down like the ancient Assyrians and took over their country.

Under these difficult circumstances Saudi Arabia was happy to agree with Bush's request that American combat troops, aircraft, and weapons be sent to help defend the desert kingdom in the event of an Iraqi invasion. The action was code-named Operation Desert Shield, and for the first time in Saudi Arabia's modern history foreign, non-Muslim troops were stationed on sacred Islamic ground.

Prodded into action by its American representative, the UN Security Council, which is responsible for threats to world peace under the UN system, reacted with equal speed. It approved Resolution 660, calling for the immediate withdrawal of Iraqi forces from Kuwait. Next, Resolution 661 imposed sanctions on all trade to and from

Iraq, including exports of Iraqi oil. In all, twelve resolutions dealing with Iraq were passed by the Security Council, the twelfth being the most important since it approved the use of force if necessary to compel Iraq to withdraw from Kuwait.

DESERT STORM

Operation Desert Storm, the follow-up to Operation Desert Shield, brought the armies of twenty-six nations together in an international coalition to defeat an aggressor nation. It was a "first" in the sense that UN forces had been involved previously only in peacekeeping operations; allowed only to defend themselves if attacked. And because the coalition armies were led by American commanders, the United States was for the first time at war with an Arab state.

The "hundred hours" of Desert Storm also brought a new kind of war to the world, one based on extremely sophisticated weapons. The Iraqi army, trained by the Russians, relied on conventional military strategy, digging a defensive perimeter of trenches three lines deep along the Saudi-Kuwait border backed by tanks and artillery, with Saddam's elite Republican Guards behind these lines in case of a breakthrough. The strategy had worked reasonably well against Iran's lightly armed human wave tactics. But the Iraqis had never faced the sophisticated weaponry of modern military technology. Day after day, hour upon hour, laser-guided jet aircraft pounded Iraqi lines, while high-level bombing raids into Iraq itself destroyed the country's roads, bridges, factories, power stations, and other targets. These raids had the additional effect of demoralizing the civilian population. Thus, some 400 Iraqis were killed when a U.S. stealth bomber guided to its target by radar attacked an air-raid shelter in a residential area of Baghdad by mistake; it had been thought to be an army command post.

Due to this vast weapons superiority the ground battles were brief. Most of Iraq's jet aircraft had been flown to Iran by their pilots for the sake of safety; they were seized by the Iranians as payment for part of the $900 million in damages to Iranian territory during the 1980–1988 war. Lacking air protection, Iraqi troops mostly broke and ran or were surrounded and forced to surrender. Behind them they left Kuwait as a burned-out shell, 600 of its 950 producing oil wells on fire and its fields littered with unexploded mines.

Some oil fires were still burning in Kuwait one year after the Persian Gulf War.

On February 27, 1991, Desert Storm ended as abruptly as it had begun. President Bush ordered a cease-fire, saying that America and the world had drawn a line in the sand by refusing to accept Iraq's aggression against Kuwait as lawful international action. With coalition forces occupying 15 percent of Iraq's territory and its army no longer effective, the prevailing belief was that Iraq was no longer a threat to its neighbors or to world peace. Saddam Hussein would soon be removed by his own people, most world leaders believed.

The events that followed the cease-fire seemed to confirm this belief. The Kurds rose in revolt and quickly seized control of most of their homeland. In southern Iraq, the Shia population turned on its Sunni masters for the first time since the 1920 revolt, capturing Basra and the holy cities of Najaf and Karbala. It seemed unnecessary to send U.S. and other coalition forces to support these uprisings. Aside from incurring casualties, the Kurds and the Shia seemed to be riding a crest of popular anger against Saddam, and in any case his army was in no condition to resist.

But Saddam Hussein has an infinite capacity for survival. He was fortunate in that world leaders detested him but could see no alternative to his leadership; without Saddam, Iraq would fall into anarchy. A U.S. diplomat said: "A weakened Saddam with a weakened army and a weakened political reputation is maybe better for us if he is in power than if he is martyred."[41]

Saddam was lucky also in that the Republican Guard had stayed out of the ground fighting and was still intact as a military force. He first turned it on the Shia; they had little in the way of modern weapons and received no support from Iran. Shia partisans made their last stand in defense of the shrines of Ali and Husayn in Najaf and Karbala but were worn down in a siege in which the shrines were severely damaged. The survivors fled into the marshes, where they were hunted down like animals, while U.S. observers watched from positions just south of the Iraqi border; their orders were to not interfere in an internal Iraqi matter.

The Kurds' uprising suffered a similar fate. Outgunned and outnumbered, and lacking outside support, the Pesh Mergas were driven from the northern cities they had just recaptured. Some two million Kurds were again refugees, fleeing into Turkey across the snowy mountains of their homeland. Their plight aroused international concern, especially with Western reporters and TV crews on the scene, and in April 1991 the Security Council approved Resolution 688, condemning Iraq's repression of its own people. The resolution also directed Iraq to allow immediate access to Kurdistan by humanitarian organizations such as the Red Cross. As a result the Bush administration organized Operation Provide Comfort. Unlike Desert Storm, it was designed for rescue rather than for military victory. American transport planes air-dropped food, clothing, tents, blankets, and medical supplies to the starving Kurds, while U.S. and British aircraft patrolled the territory with orders to shoot down Iraqi planes if they interfered.

The humanitarian aid stopped after most of the refugees returned to their villages, but the air cover has continued up to the present. In this manner Iraqi Kurdistan down to the 36th parallel of latitude has become a "no-fly" zone, with Iraqi planes and forces prohibited from entering. A similar no-fly zone was marked out for southern Iraq, up to the 32nd parallel, to protect the Shia population from further repression. Thus, in effect, Iraq has been outlawed from the world of nations, having been deprived of sovereignty over a large part of its territory due to actions contrary to international law and relations with other nations.

AT WAR WITH THE WORLD

As noted in the Introduction, Iraq's reputed possession of chemical and biological weapons and its efforts to develop a nuclear bomb have become a major concern for the international community. Use of these weapons against Iranian soldiers and its own Kurdish population on several occasions was well documented, in the latter case being clearly a form of genocide. The revelations prompted the Security Council to set up UNSCOM (UN Special Commission on Iraq's Weapons of Mass Destruction), charged with locating and destroying these weapons. Resolution 713 set up a UN monitoring system, with a team of inspectors from various countries who would proceed to Iraq to ensure destruction of the weapons. When these inspectors were satisfied that this had been done, the sanctions on Iraq would be lifted. The assumption was that the Iraqi weapons could be located with relative ease, due to their concentration in certain types of industries such as pharmaceutical plants. Once the elimination had been completed, Iraq would become a fourth-rate power, no longer a threat to its neighbors or to world peace.

Eight years after UNSCOM was set up and the inspection team began its work, its mission was yet to be completed. As a result, Iraq remains an outlaw nation. The relationship between Saddam and the inspectors has been described as a cat-and-mouse game, with Saddam playing (for him) the unlikely role of the mouse. As the UN inspectors fanned out across the land between the rivers they found evidence of chemical and biological weapons production in unlikely places—private homes, chicken coops, research labs, vaccine-making and drug factories, even beer and dairy plants. But despite Iraq's insistence that it has complied with UN requirements and destroyed all its weapons of mass destruction, many of them and the materials used to make them are still unaccounted for.

Up until 1996 the international community of nations had stood firmly united against Saddam and his country. In that year, however, the Iraqi leader accepted UN Security Council Resolution 986. Subject to continued access by the inspection team to all parts of Iraq for verification purposes, it allows Iraq to sell 700,000 barrels per day of oil over a six-month period in order to buy urgently needed food and medicines. Saddam had previously rejected the resolution as a violation of the country's sovereignty, since it limited Iraq's right to control its national resources. But with European oil companies and corporations eager to help Iraq repair its battered economy and make profits in the process, it has become increasingly difficult for the United States as leader of the anti-Iraq coalition to keep the sanctions in place.

Unfortunately, the country's outlaw status and war with the world have brought little relief to the ordinary Iraqi people. Their children are the most affected, with extreme shortages of medicines and medical equipment and limited food supplies creating almost an underfed and malnourished generation. The Clinton administration on two occasions, in 1998 and 1999, was barely dissuaded from large-scale bombing attacks on Baghdad, and periodic clashes between Iraqi aircraft and American planes patrolling the no-fly zones pose a continual risk of escalating conflict into a wider war.

What are the prospects for the land between the rivers? Can it ever recover its ancient prosperity and peaceful existence? What would it take to establish workable democratic institutions, a free press, freedom of dissent, free elections, and a national legislature like the U.S. Congress that would allow representation by the various groups composing Iraqi society? And most important, what would be the alternative to Saddam Hussein? The U.S. Congress in 1999 allocated $97 million for the overthrow of the Ba'th leader, but as a former associate of his, now in exile, remarked, "We all have a little Saddam in us; we are a brutal people." The opposition to Saddam has yet to unite in a common program of action, and Britain's policy of working with Sunni merchants, tribal leaders, and an imported monarchy failed to develop anything resembling representative government.

Whatever its defects as an imperial power, the Ottoman empire brought peace and stability to Iraq, along with much of the Middle East. It did so through indirect rule, periodic but not heavy taxation, religious toleration, and a sort of disinterested benevolence. The United States since 1991 has said that the Gulf must be defended because of our "national interest" in the security of that region.

But our defense of this "national interest" in a distant region has involved massive deployment of military and naval forces at enormous expense. It may well be that involvement may eventually prove counterproductive, as the United States finds itself isolated in its single-minded Iraq policy. In that case either the Ottoman model or some form of benevolent trusteeship may, in the long run, bring peace and stability to the land between the rivers. The proud people of Iraq deserve no less.

SOURCE NOTES

1. Abba Eban, *Diplomacy for the Next Century*. New Haven: Yale University Press, 1998, p. 35.

2. Ofra Bengio, *Saddam's Word: Political Discourse in Iraq*. New York: Oxford University Press, 1998, p. 69.

3. Eban, *op. cit.*, p. 176.

4. Gavin Young, *Iraq: Land of Two Rivers*. London: Collins, 1980.

5. Mike Edwards, "Eyewitness Iraq," *National Geographic*, 196, 5, November 1999, p. 8.

6. Ronald Sack, *Images of Nebuchadnezzar*. Selinsgrove, PA: Susquehanna University Press, 1991, pp. 83–84.

7. There are various accounts of this experience. See M.A. Salihi, *Muhammad: Man and Prophet*. Rockport MA: Element Books, 1995, pp. 63–64, and Martin Lings, *Muhammad*. London: George Allen & Unwin, 1983, pp. 44–45.

8. Akbar S. Ahmed, *Discovering Islam*. London: Routledge & Kegan Paul, 1988, p. 34.

9. "The Ghazi is the instrument of God; he purifies the earth from the faith of polytheism; he is the sword of God, protector and refuge of believers." Paul Wittek, *Rise of the Ottoman Empire*. London: Royal Asiatic Society, 1965, p. 14.

10. Tareq Ismael, *Iraq and Iran: Roots of Conflict*. Syracuse: Syracuse University Press, 1982, pp. 5–8.

11. Reeva Simon, *Iraq Between the Two World Wars.* New York: Columbia University Press, 1986, p. 4.

12. Gertrude Bell was one of a number of "intrepid English-women" who journeyed without escort or protection into the wild male-dominated desert lands of the Middle East in the nineteenth and early twentieth centuries. She was instrumental in the establishment of Iraq within its present borders due to her intimate knowledge of the land and its people, especially the tribal chiefs. See the biography by Janet Wallach, *Desert Queen: The Extraordinary Life of Gertrude Bell.* New York: Doubleday, 1996; Bell's Letters, *The Letters of Gertrude Bell.* New York: Boni & Liveright, 1927; and other references for details of her life.

13. Mohammed A. Tarbush, *The Role of the Military in Politics: A Case Study of Iraq to 1941.* London: Kegan Paul International, 1982, p. 185.

14. Muhammad Habib al-'Ubaidi, quoted in Tarbush, *op. cit.,* p. 40.

15. Phebe Marr, *History of Modern Iraq.* London: Longman's, 1983, p. 160.

16. Maurice Peterson, *Both Sides of the Curtain.* London: Constable, 1950, p. 138.

17. K.S. Husry, "The Assyrian Affair of 1933," *International Journal of Middle East Studies,* 5, 1974, p. 166.

18. Hanna Batatu, *The Old Social Classes and the Revolutionary Movements of Iraq.* Princeton: Princeton University Press, 1978, p. 28.

19. Speech to the General Assembly, April 29, 1947, reported in *The New York Times,* April 30, 1947.

20. Samira Hajj, *The Making of Iraq 1900–1963.* Albany: SUNY Press, Chapter 5. The name Qassem, in Arabic, means "he who divides and rules."

21. Lora Lukitz, *Iraq: The Search for National Identity.* London: Frank Cass, 1995, p. 130.

22. Quoted in Bernard Vernier, *Iraq Today* (L'Irak Aujourd'hui). Paris: 1963, p. 196.

23. Edmund Ghareeb, *The Kurdish Question in Iraq*. Syracuse: Syracuse University Press, 1981, p. 98.

24. Marr, *op. cit.*, p. 168.

25. Ghareeb, *op. cit.*, p. 112.

26. Derek Hopwood et al., *Iraq: Power and Society*. Reading, UK: Ithaca Press, 1963, p. 76.

27. Marion and Peter Sluglett, *Iraq Since 1958: From Revolution to Dictatorship*. London: Kegan Paul International, 1987, p. 188.

28. Hopwood, *op. cit.*, p. 67.

29. Elaine Sciolino, *The Outlaw State*. New York: John Wiley, 1991, p. 83.

30. Ofra Bengio, *Saddam's Word: Political Discourse in Iraq*. London: Oxford University Press, 1988, p. 24.

31. Sciolino, p. 89.

32. Bengio, *op. cit.*, pp. 27-28.

33. Sciolino, *op. cit.*, p. 99.

34. Bengio, *loc. cit.*

35. Sciolino, p. 128.

36. Human Rights Watch, *Iraq's Circle of Genocide: The Anfal Campaign Against the Kurds*. New Haven: Yale University Press, 1995, pp. 4–5. "Anfal" is the Arabic name of the eighth *sura* (chapter) of the Koran. It first appeared as a revelation to Muhammad after the victory at Badr, where 319 Muslims routed a force of 1,000 Meccan unbelievers, and was viewed by them as proof that God was on their side.

37. Fouad Ajami, *The Dream Palace of the Arabs*. New York: Pantheon Books, 1998, pp. 171–172.

38. Ofra Bengio, *Saddam Speaks on the Gulf Crisis: A Collection of Documents*. Tel Aviv, Israel: Shiloah Institute, Tel Aviv University, 1992, p. 99.

39. Ajami, *op. cit.*, p. 166.

40. Bengio, *Saddam Speaks*, p. 122.

41. Stephen Kinzer, in *The New York Times*, December 27, 1998.

SUGGESTED READINGS

Ahmed, Akbar S. *Discovering Islam*. London: Routledge & Kegan Paul, 1988.

Ali, Omar. *Crisis in the Arabian Gulf: An Independent Iraqi Perspective*. Westport, CT: Praeger, 1993.

Axelgard, Fred W. *Iraq in Transition*. Boulder, CO: Westview Press, 1986.

Baram, Amatzia. *Culture, History and Ideology in the Formation of Ba'thist Iraq, 1968–1969*. New York: St. Martin's Press, 1991.

Bulloch, John, and Harvey Morris. *Saddam's War: Origins of the Kuwait Conflict*. London: Faber and Faber, 1991.

Crawford, Harriet. *Sumer and the Sumerians*. Cambridge: Cambridge University Press, 1991.

Darwish, Adel. *Unholy War: The Secret History of Saddam's War.* London: Victor Gollancz, 1991.

Fuller, Graham. *Iraq in the Next Decade*. Santa Monica, CA: Rand Corporation, 1993.

Ghareeb, Edmund. *The Kurdish Question in Iraq*. Syracuse: Syracuse University Press, 1981.

Hajj, Samira. *The Making of Iraq 1955–1963*. Albany: SUNY Press, 1997.

136 Hawley, T. M. *Against the Fires of Hell: The Environmental Disaster of the Gulf War.* New York: Harcourt Brace Jovanovich, 1992.

Hopwood, Derek and others, eds. *Iraq: Power and Society.* Reading, UK: Ithaca Press, 1991.

Kaikobad, Karijan. *The Shatt al-Arab Boundary Question.* London: Oxford University Press, 1988.

Kienlo, Eberhard. *Ba'th v. Ba'th: The Conflict Between Syria and Iraq.* London: I. B. Tauris, 1990.

Laizer, Sherri. *Martyrs, Traitors and Patriots: Kurdistan After the Gulf War.* London: Zed Books, 1996.

Lukitz, Lora. *Iraq: The Search for National Identity.* London: Frank Cass, 1995.

Makiya, Kanan. *Republic of Fear.* New York: Norton, 1993. First published in 1989 by the University of California Press under the author's pseudonym of Samir al-Khalil.

Marr, Phebe. *A History of Modern Iraq.* London: Longman's, 1983.

McDowall, David. *A Modern History of the Kurds.* London: I. B. Tauris, 1996.

Moore, John Norton. *Crisis in the Gulf: Enforcing the Rule of Law.* New York: Oceana Publications, 1992.

Morony, Michael. *Iraq After the Muslim Conquest.* Princeton: Princeton University Press, 1984.

Mufti, Malik. *Sovereign Creations: Pan-Arabism and Political Order in Syria and Lebanon.* Ithaca: Cornell University Press, 1996.

Nakash, Yitzhak. *The Shi'is of Iraq.* Princeton: Princeton University Press, 1994.

Nemet-Nejat, Karen Rhea. *Daily Life in Ancient Mesopotamia.* Westport, CT: Greenwood Press, 1998.

Postgate, J. N. *Early Mesopotamia.* London: Routledge and Kegan Paul, 1994.

Rezun, Miron. *Saddam Hussein's Gulf Wars.* Westport, CT: Praeger, 1992.

Silverfarb, Daniel. *The Twilight of British Ascendancy in Iraq 1941–1950*. New York: St. Martin's Press, 1994.

Simon, Reeva. *Iraq Between Two World Wars*. New York: Columbia University Press, 1986.

Sluglett, Marion, and Peter Sluglett. *Iraq Since 1958: From Revolution to Dictatorship*. London: Kegan Paul International, 1987.

Ta'uber, Eliezer. *The Formation of Modern Syria and Iraq*. London: Frank Cass, 1995.

Workman, W. Thorn. *The Social Origins of the Gulf War*. Boulder, CO: Lynne Rienner Publishers, 1994.

BASIC FACTS ABOUT IRAQ

Location: Middle East, borders on Iran, Jordan, Saudi Arabia, Syria, Turkey

Area: 167,924 square miles (434,924 sq km), slightly larger than California

Capital: Baghdad (pop.: 3,400,000); other major cities are Basra and Mosul

Population: 21,722,287 (1998 estimate)

Annual Population Growth Rate: 3.2%

Rural/Urban Population Ratio: 20%/70%

Ethnic Divisions: 75–80% Arab, 15–20% Kurdish; small Jewish, Armenian, and other groups

Major Languages: Arabic, Kurdish; English widely understood

Life Expectancy at Birth: 66 years (male), 65 years (female)

Death Rate per 1,000 Population: 66/1,000 (estimate only, may be higher due to UN sanctions)

Infant Mortality Rate per 1,000 Population: 108/1,000 in south and central areas; 72/1,000 in northern (Kurdish) area

139

Physicians Available: one per 1,922 persons (1999)

Religions: 62% Shia Muslim, 35% Sunni Muslim, 3% Jewish, Christian, etc.

Adult Literacy Rate: 70.7% males, 45% females

Type of Government: officially a republic; in reality a single-party state under an absolute ruler

Independence Date: October 5, 1932 as kingdom; July 17, 1958, as republic

Head of State: Saddam Hussein, who also serves as secretary-general of the ruling Ba'th party and head of the Revolution Command Council (RCC)

Legislature: (authorized by temporary constitution) a single-chamber National Assembly of 250 seats, 220 elected by popular vote and 30 appointed by the president for 4-year terms

Political Parties: none legal except the Ba'th

Suffrage: universal at age 18 (males and females)

Climate and Topography: mostly desert, with mild to cool winters and dry hot summers; cold winters with heavy snow in Kurdish mountain areas; elevation ranges from sea level to 3,608 meters (12,000 feet)

Natural Resources: oil, natural gas, phosphates, sulfur, lead, gypsum

Agricultural Crops: wheat, barley, rice, cotton, dates

Industry: oil refineries, petrochemical complexes, textile and cement plants

Economic Development: no details available due to UN sanctions, but reportedly much of the revenues from the oil-for-food program has been siphoned off for construction projects and repairs to damaged oil refineries

Currency ($U.S. equivalent): 2,080 dinars = $1

Inflation Rate: Estimated at 6,000%

INDEX

Page numbers in *italics* refer to illustrations.

141